Words of One, Volume Five

Words of One.

Volume Five

By Sophia Love

ISBN – 978-1-7371185-0-3

All books published by Off World Publications ©

www.amazon.com/author/sophialove

Cover illustration by Tom Wundrak, Fine Art

Other Works

The Guardian, 2016

Inclusion, 2017

sī bôrg, 2017

Join me on a Love Quest, 2018

The Imposter, 2019

Words of One. All Volumes, 2020/2021

Visit *www.sophialove.org* for these and more.

Table of Contents

Introduction

You hold the transcription of an ongoing conversation with the being I have come to identify as One. It is written here as it was heard telepathically. These conversations have been going on since 2012. They are shared now due to their current focus; this extraordinary year we navigate together. Use your discernment with them, please. Since you've found your way to these pages, there is more than likely some benefit for you in reading them.

Subsequent conversations will be shared in future Volumes.

With blessings and love,
Sophia
2020.5.31

"This journey continues and takes us ever deeper into truths and methods for the creation of the Matrix. Allow these words to inform your awareness of what life has been here for you. These words tell your past. You will define your future. Humanity rises now to write the rest of the story as fully conscious beings. Informed choice is reinforced with truth. That truth is found in these words."

One
2021.4.20

Foreword

Since this text is the transcription of a conversation, it is crucial to clarify in what ways the text has been interpreted to convey emphasis and voice. There are several of these cues, and they are as follows:

Bold face emphasis is used for extra stress on specific words. These are not my interpretations of what I heard, but highlighted that way as it came through.

Italics indicate my own voice (that is, Sophia). Unless otherwise noted, all regular font face body text is the voice of One.

Footnotes and brackets may also be used during the One's dialogue to clarify contextual confusions.

Chapter 1. January

Words of One

January 21, 2021

It is the One.

I will share with you plans and outlines of plans in order to keep you informed, but not compromised. These are not to be shared. Not yet, and not until all plans have been executed and the United States of America is restored to her intended hierarchy of diplomacy.

This will not be tomorrow or immediately. This will be months from now, and at that point this conversation is to be shared. Included in the fifth book as it were. For there are more books on the way, and words to be shared.

Now then.

A new plan is formulated now. There was a glitch in the process and it concerned those people who are loyal supporters of truth. People who are, what you would call innocent bystanders to the drama playing out on planet earth and headquartered in your capitol section of the country.

This unexpected delay occurred because of a single button that could not be sewn up. It concerned the military. There are factions within whom give their allegiance to not their oath or the people but an ideology. These are armed citizens/military guardsmen. You heard of the sweep through just days before the scheduled inauguration, of somehow a "loyalty check" of the troops in Washington DC. This sweep was begun, and there is much mis-information about it, to check for capabilities and intents. There were indications of infiltration and a plan to mow down any who reportedly came under the spotlight of a soldier supporting a specific agenda.

There were not many. The signal was to be the arrests. The gathering would have been plentiful enough to take down all of the major players. This was a surprise attack, meant to be a surprise attack. It would have created chaos as military would have been filmed firing on specific and their own. Also, on government officials. What it was akin to, but not exactly like, was the taking of a suicide pill rather than confess.

There were a few in the know.

The many would have been lost as victims and in the mayhem, there would be no formal conclusion or "outing" so that the public would know why. It would not have been orderly.

These were only a few.

There was also a bomb. Its whereabouts could not be determined. The triggering event was the EBS broadcast. The triggering event was the EBS broadcast.

It was attempted to root out the few who would have fired on their own. Information was not complete. There was no way to ensure that it wasn't going to be a bloodbath.

It was delayed to protect innocent bystanders and also prevent an eruption of war that would have occurred. It would be months before it was clear who did what and why. The country would have been under martial law the entire time.

Words of One

The bomb, if there is one, has not been found.

The soldiers have been. As was said, there were only a few.

What will occur, will happen, will begin in numerous locations, and be heard on your devices. You will be informed.

But; and here is the crucial difference, you will be informed **after** arrests have been made. These will occur under cover of darkness and possible weekends/off hours. These will occur **before** the reasons for them are announced to the public.

You will be told who.
You will be told why.
You will be told when.
You will be told how.

These telling's will go on and on and be repeated – you, in the United States of America, will wake up to the telling's.

As the United States of America goes, so goes the world. The awareness of dark intent, intent not made public before being put into "office", is becoming clear. This fact wakes up many and as the numbers of you demanding and desiring truth increases – **truth is rushed in as response.**

You will witness a telling of which there is no predecessor. You will see the admission of evidence that will be impossible to forget. You will witness the desperation and ultimately face a choice. That choice will be – do I still hold what I was told **before these revelations** as true? Or. Do I trust my eyes and ears and inner compass to now discern what is truth?

The next operation is a sting, yet not as satisfying for many of you. Plans had to be altered and there were addendums made to accommodate the filming of and locations of the players. This is a logistical process and not a correction or a change of plans. This was a possibility that was seen, yes.

It held a lower probability in this seeing, and until the threat became concrete, or as an actual possibility, it was not accurately planned for.

No-one wanted to halt the process and therefore it is not to be halted. It has changed.

It still looms into the very near future on your earth, and in your country.

Know this – it remains a surprise now, even to those on the inside and in the military. There is only one who will pull the trigger on this, and until that moment it will not happen.

There will be no leaks of information. You will not know in advance.

It will happen sooner rather than later and this is a fact that you can count on.

It must surprise everyone.

It will be offered an assist from other-worldly events. Timing is everything.

Words of One

Before it completes the announcements and freeing of your earth, you will all know what occurred here.

There is meant to be divine intervention and a halt to this current reality matrix. Once the matrix is halted – your new world is fully visible. There has to be an acceptance of the current world as controlled matrix before that can occur.

There has to be a complete thought in order to fully birth your new earth – a full comprehension of sovereignty – freedom – individual and collective light.

You will have no "reveals" before the next step. There will be no insiders to tell you what happens next.

You are what remains. The creators of your new world, having hit rock bottom, now in dashed expectations for release.

It is your collective acceptance of freedom as the only option for fully free beings of light, that creates it. **You must view it, see it, feel it and experience it as the only option.** It then becomes your reality.

Your emotions incite a massive shift and push now for truth. Any last moment "delays" or "obstacles" or "fears" are only possible in a place that holds only the control matrix as more powerful than self.

How many more of you are there now, who see the folly of the puppet show – who see the strings? Who disregard them as real or effective?

You have become fearless. It is a necessary step before pure love manifests.

There is but a brief inhale of breath before this next obvious movement occurs. It takes you all by surprise.

There is no loss perceived in either power or eventual outcome. Indeed, a more perfect union of intent, belief, freedom and fortitude emerges now.

You will see. You will not be disappointed.

You will see, dear human, you will see.

That is all.

Thank you.

Words of One

Chapter 2. February

Words of One

February 8, 2021

It is the One.

These next moments are times of great turmoil and tumult. If you look into the specific meaning of these words, you will see that they indicate a rocking of what has been previously steady.

I will say here that a great deal of effort and control has been inserted into this reality, by those controlling the switches, in order to have a level of calm maintained and portrayed.

The hands on those switches have changed and moved further along down chains of command. What happens when this movement occurs is that those who hold the controls do not hold the full picture or have the same experience and/or stomach to hold steady. As their grip loosens, confusion increases and the illusion of reality gets fuzzier and fuzzier. Coordination of components is one of the first things to go.

The reason this is brought up today is that you are so very close. For those of you growing weary of these words, it will not be much longer where you'll be wishing for these days of waiting for their calmness and relative quiet.

What comes next will be quite a bit louder.

There are reasons for secrecy as to specifics. There are informants with truth and some with intentional falsehoods. Without specifics and subsequent disappointments, your energy can no longer be harvested.

Comprehend that in the next phase, your new earth, the higher frequency is in fact another assumption of truth.

What is currently held as true is the structure holding your reality in place today.

To use your terminology, "5D" is here already. You go there in your dreams. What you will have to get your arms around is that you wake each morning to another dream – not reality.

Reality is what you decide is real. Once you decide love holds a greater amplitude than fear – you are there.

It is simple and challenging, hence the reason you've agreed to participate at all.

The nature of what comes next is perhaps most shocking to those among you who firmly held onto the notion of 3D being the only solid truth.

You'll see new things, every bit as solid as before, that do not fit in this currently accepted construct.

Not comfortably.

And yet they exist and will not be able to be denied.

Remember what was said about the holders of the switches earlier. They are becoming shakier and shakier and thus, so is the manuscript they attempt to follow, to hold in place.

Words of One

People are forgetting their lines. In some cases, people are ad-libbing. This was never part of the plan.

What happens eventually, is a return to base instincts and values. As these are exposed, "who is who" becomes obvious. By this is meant not only individual people, but individual structures, institutions, companies, laws and governments.

It will be a mess for a while.

The over-whelming truth, the truth that rises to the surface and is ultimately obvious to the entire population, is the lynch-pin of the divine plan.

Trust this to be so.

There is chaos before, yet not for long, and then your new world is fortified with absolute truth.

This emerges in every language and land. It is heard by every person and comprehended by every life form.

It exists now, yet for most of you as a briefly remembered dream before waking.

The day approaches when you'll wake to it, hear and see and feel it in every state you find yourself.

Infuse love into whatever happens in your current day to day. In this way, the transition is sped up and smoother. You will see the "unbelievable" only in the realm of your currently accepted construct. You've been taught to believe as well as not to believe.

Everything is challenged now.

Everything comes unhinged now.

You are here now to show the way to a new door, with new hinges, and they are fastened with truth, and held on with love. This is why you are here now and you will discover quickly your purpose.

Trust your truth.

Things shift quickly now, and you are meant to be a solid bit of foundation for others who need one. Together you create your new world, not alone.

It is Oneness that actualizes the new Earth.

Oneness is truth.

That is all.

Thank you.

Words of One

Sophia, it is the One.

There are things to say.

These concern the entire notion of government. It is an idea that sets in place positions of unequal power and of rule. It is a false notion, not held up by sovereignty, but instead fully supported in a false construct.

Government was not meant to be carried out by the same people for decades of years. Not in the country you occupy. Not in the United States.

There is a higher purpose here, as was laid out at its beginning. That purpose is one of Unity. That purpose grew from groups of people occupying different sections of land while close together on the same land form. It was an idea intended to promote cooperation, trade, and mutual interest when other, more centrist powers were interfering, i.e., England.

Government, in this case, was public service. It was something many people took a turn at for a short while.

It was done because someone had to help coordinate trade and surplus and roads. It was considered civic responsibility and it was shared by everyone able to do so.

Government was not initially considered occupation. It was civic responsibility. It was set up this way so that Unity could be physically realized. Many groups of you, separated by climate, crops and location, working together as one united entity.

Protecting citizen rights was primary.

Each group of people/eventually each state had a common purpose and that was to live independent of outside control. The government of these United States as well as many other "countries" have morphed into rule and control by elitist factions. These have been put in place by earth's controllers over time and no place on earth is there an exception.

It's for this reason that you are about to see the earth's governments crumble and change. New forms will be necessary, are required, for the new earth. Control, conquer and ownership are not sustained in this incoming frequency. They are like castles in the sand on the beach, waiting for the tide to roll in. It is coming.

It will help you to remember, as chaos ensues, that the sand remains and castles can be rebuilt in new places and with new methods. Perhaps they won't be necessary at all. Man will ultimately decide how he and she will "govern" themselves. Much depends on climate, custom, resources. All depends on choice.

Your existing structures will not withstand this next wave. If they do, know that they are meant to. In no place of your new earth does there exist any form of slavery, duplicity, abuse or mis-use of life.

In no place does the horror continue.

Words of One

The horror, however, has to be rounded up and exposed. Seen so that it can no longer hide. This job is a massive one. It is carried out now by man, as it must be, as man participated in its creation.

I know many of you wished for a divine or "beyond earth" hand in removing the most dreadful of practices for you. There is help for this, yet realize if it were taken over by an outside force, the effect would be altered. It would be akin to turning in a science fair project that your older brother made for you. Perhaps it wins prizes, but they turn out to be hollow and for show only.

The work to free mankind is the work of humanity. It has to be this way so that its effects become part of the genetic code here. Freedom is an inside job.

As man has an inclination to subservience and obedience, man also has a drive for independence. It is this drive that pushes forward now and carries the race. It is freedom which equates to love, and rests as the base for Oneness. Love unites, while fear separates.

Love does not unite by fear or force but with connection, compassion and truth. There are few questions needed in any formal decisions put forth when governing self or other. These are:

"Is this coming from love or fear?"
"Does it allow freedom or curtail and constrain?"
"Does it promote life and vitality or infiltrate and negate those things?"

With these thoughts as a basis for any necessary governing bodies, citizens will not require law degrees but common sense and self-respect in order to be effective.

There is an expression that states that the most effective leaders are not those who have the most followers, but those who inspire the most leaders.

History will prove this to be true for these United States and many other of your current territories.

Your world begins its global change of structure now, to one that coincides with New Earth frequencies.

It will appear messy for a while, but not for too long. Humanity is anxious for change and the resonance cooperates with man to see this accomplished.

You are in for quite a show. Remember this is a re-structure and not merely a destruction of this current society. This will help you to tolerate the mess lying about and perhaps encourage you to help pick up the pieces and put them together in a new way. One that cooperates with your New Earth, encourages love, and guarantees freedom.

Your new world is astounding, dear human, and you are building her yourselves.

You are in for such a treat.

That is all.

Thank you.

Words of One

February 10, 2021

Sophia, it is the One.

Hello. Thank you.

I have some questions.

I know that you do.

They concern what occurs now for the race, and on the planet. Also, something that you said to me almost 6 months ago now. (see footnote below)

Yes. Go ahead then.

What I see now is a level of depression in the people. A feeling of "how will we ever come out of this?" There are babies who have been in lockdown for most of their lives, who haven't seen other children for a year. People have given up hope in many cases. The toll on the psyche is a real one. There is frequent talk about needing an "act of God". Then, there is what you said to me in August of last year – that help would come after the crimes against humanity were revealed, and humanity somehow found forgiveness in their hearts for the perpetrators of those crimes. This was what I comprehended from what you said.

Will you respond to these things with information on where we are now in this scenario?

Thank you.

There are truths yet to be revealed, facts to be exposed on a mass scale. There are unknowns that need to be known. It is not the plan that man suffer endlessly, but that man sees the truth of his existence at all, so that he holds full awareness. Then, he holds full knowledge and can make a choice about suffering.

What does that mean? "Make a choice about suffering". To be human in this current atmosphere is equivalent to suffering. Truth is not anywhere clear — not about the virus or the vaccines or the mask and lockdown protocols or the real force driving these circumstances. By their very nature they cause suffering in the race. The race has no choice but to experience suffering.

All suffering is fear based. Once truth emerges, humanity will have a choice about fear. Once humanity sees that these circumstances are not dealt them by random, but rather by a race of beings who declare ownership over them — anger will replace suffering and action will replace helpless and/or hopeless. This is where man chooses.

Truth is emerging now in many pockets. There is about to be a flood.

The first choice is whether to believe the news brought by this flood. It will wash away the falsehoods and the race will be left with little to hang on to, other than this new information as presented.

Once belief sets in, the second choice is how to respond to these truths, these crimes against the race.

This clean-up of trafficking operations is intense, and ongoing. By the time man is presented with the choice, they (*meaning the human trafficking operations*) will have been exposed and eradicated. It is a huge effort, one that has enlisted help from beyond your earth. This is the help spoken of earlier. The help unseen by you in the

31

general public, but very real. This is the assistance.

Many of you on planet right now, also assist in other realms. You are active in your dream state. All of this as real as what occurs on your nightly news casts, perhaps more so.

The reason for this overwhelming grief and sense of loss, is for this "invisible uncovering" of human trafficking and massive suffering. **It is felt by all of you.** It has become so evident now, the numbers so large, that all of you feel it. All of you sense the horror and desperation of your fellow man.

You actually have more than one question before you in all of this. It is what to do about the humans carrying out and continuing these crimes, as well as how to stop them permanently at their source. It is the answer to both that frees the race and allows it to move on.

The beings who now lose control here, will have to be stopped and removed. They will not do this of their own accord as it is not in their make-up. They are not human. It is this aspect of the current operation where help from beyond the race assists you now. This will continue until all factions are removed.

There are many more humans involved and here is where mankind chooses what to do with them.

As it always proceeds in 3D – first there are thoughts and then the actions take place as manifestations of those thoughts. Much of the process is unconscious.

The knowing of the level of pain is arduous and awful. It was chosen to be presented gradually, felt gradually, as to avoid too much shock. It is done this way so the race has the best chance at survival.

Emotions run your world, and create your environment. You are/mankind is waiting for outside help and praying for intervention. It arrives and assists now as these beings who control the trafficking are removed. There is "invisible" help already.

Yet you seek visible help.

I tell you this.

It comes in a way unexpected and will, when it arrives, serve as answers to all of man's questions.

Your world exists within an aspect of "time" where it is necessary to witness a play-by-play process in order to be believed. This, you live through now. It feels interminable, yet compared to the many prior eras and thousands of years, it is but a moment.

Man has to feel this fully, and in this way, even without being an active player in the discovery and eradication of human trafficking systems – he does. He feels their suffering in an unconscious and very literal sense now. Words like hopeless and helpless are indicators.

You are One.

There has been a great portion of your connection hidden from you. It is about to be revealed and you already feel it. This explains some of the reasons for the despair you see now, expressed in so

Words of One

many others and so many places.

You all feel first what you are about to see. It is a process.

This part is not forever. It is a lead-in to visual awareness.

You will make decisions then, about what to do, with full comprehension.

The goal is a fully informed race; conscious unity. You are almost there.

That is all that will be said on this day.

Thank you.[1]

---

[1]

Here is part of the conversation from August 2020, as referenced. It is found in Words of One. Volume III:

It is I; it is One.

The proof you seek comes not wrapped in human skin, but other ways, other skin, other locations. It does not travel your traffic pattern or route, actually. Not ever and not now. It must be summoned.

Would you summon it?
This is beyond torturous. It has split the very fabric of my life. It is ripping me apart.

I can, Sophia, and I will. Just not yet.

Then I cannot continue. Your refusal to summon assistance for a dying populace is cruel. If help is available that is. Else, what you've done is create a facade of freedom that never intended to manifest. That is something I will not do. I will not participate in this.

Why have you done this? What is the purpose of you contacting me?

The purpose has always been redemption.

Of who?

Of those who would deceive and operate solely for self.

Who does that???

You make it sound as if this whole thing is orchestrated by you, for a select few – That our pain matters not – That until they turn over and figure it out it...

WAIT. STOP. IS THAT IT?

They are human and this is true.

We will not receive help until they seek redemption?
(I was shaking here, as the gravity of what was said was sinking in and being realized.)

Not all of them, but many and specific of them.

Are you f**** kidding me? They will not admit to their crimes! They will be hung, or worse...**

This is the part where humanity enters.

What. Are. You. Saying.

That the race must stop the activity, yes. But love anyway.

Words of One

Once that happens, they will stop on their own.
The fear is at an all-time high now, from every angle and all sides. It needs to subside.

It will not subside until there is help given. The violence is worsening and becoming more and more visual.
It approaches chaos.
We are breaking apart.

You will not be permitted to break. You'll see.
Something will occur.

Please. Stop with the forecasting.

You will come together and forgiveness will override the fear.
Once that occurs, redemption is sought. And then help comes.

February 12, 2021

It is the One.

There are facts about things and people that you are not being told. Here is one of the reasons that confusion reigns right now.

The frequency, the current incoming frequency, supports and exposes your more intuitive and telepathic nature. It emerges in these energies, whether or not you recognize it.

How this will manifest, is in a sharper recognition of untruth and/or deliberate misrepresentation. When these things are encountered, they won't "feel right". They will not be as easily accepted as they were before. The addition of a title, position or degree will not alter the feeling of false narrative. No one will have to tell you this, it will be a visceral experience.

There are those actors who've spent lives on the big screen, and are good at putting on a show. It will be a more polished performance with them and their words may be believed a while longer because of it. Included here are news media anchors. Yet even they, who read lines from a prompter and act sincere, will be felt as either true or not true. They will feel this themselves.

Many of you are concerned about your friends and family, who may still believe in something you do not. What you see as blatant efforts at distortion. You needn't be (concerned). The change in frequency takes care of this, not only for themselves, but eventually for the people they quote and listen to.

It will, rather quickly now, become impossible to unknowingly report and support blatant un-truths. Those that continue, will be "selling out their soul" in a sense, in order to do so. This is a planned program for control of the race, of the story, of the performance.

These actors and news anchors will not be able to continue feeding lies to their audience without feeling the consequences personally.

It's important to realize that there are layers of deceit. Some, willingly take it on as performance for the thrill and the paycheck.

Others, honestly, do not know the machine behind their script and make-up. They are performers, and they consider what they do an art form. It is all they know, or else something they've wanted to do their entire lives. They've not considered or looked beyond their acting – to the effect of what they do.

They've not looked past the applause. They've not looked past the paycheck. They will begin to, as the frequency changes.

What is being said here today is that even in this age of monopoly media with a uniform intent – it takes humans to put it forth and humans to believe it. Humans are not robots.

At the end of the day, you either trust or distrust a person, and that informs your belief system. All of you are both feeling and changed by – these new frequencies.

You may not specifically identify what is happening as an uptick in telepathy, yet what you'll experience will feel like knowing things without hearing them said aloud. Knowing things from another person directly.

You won't know **how** you know, yet you won't doubt **that** you know.

This change heralds the beginning of universal truth.

It is the reason that you do not have to worry about the story or how it ends. It does so with everyone on the same page, having the same information.

You know, and are aware of discrepancies to the social narrative early perhaps. Yet, this does not mean you'll always hold separate facts as truth. There will come a day when there will one set of facts. These will be the ones heard and told by everyone.

Trust that the plan for the awakening is comprehensive and handles every circumstance. No one will be left without being given every option and all pieces of truth.

It is a self-driven process. You travel on different roads, at different speeds. Yet, all roads lead to truth, awareness, awakening and full consciousness. This illusion is exposed for all to see. Once you believe that, you can focus on your purpose.

Be the light from which others utilize to discover their own. This is your purpose, humanity's purpose always.

It was always the plan and why you do this together, as One.

There are/there will be no stones left unturned. No one left behind. No horrors remaining hidden.

Words of One

This is your expansion. Trust the process.

Feel into the changes within and allow.

That is all.

Thank you.

Goodbye, Sophia, my chosen one.

February 18, 2021
4:30 AM

Parts of this conversation were personal. Included here are excerpts for everyone.

Emerging truths are to be seen and heard and considered, eventually. The conversation changes.

When?

It takes a while.

Why did I hear "March" and then hesitation, and then "May"?

There is more than one conversation.

What changes initially are conversations about your government. The farcical nature of the **currently sitting president** becomes obvious. Facts about the **corruption and fraud** emerge quickly and are recognized.

These are followed with **personal treason and deeply disturbing facts and charges. The plot is revealed,** and this is not by your current media, but **by an outside event.** This happens **soon.**

I honestly can't take "soon". Please be more specific. I will ask specific things now.

When will the truth about the fraud in the election be public knowledge?

Will it be clear it was another country?

Words of One

Yes.

Eventually names and the money trail are released.

When?

Late March – possibly April.

Will we have a sitting President?

The military holds the power for a while.

Does DJT return as President?

Under different and brand-new circumstances, he does, yes.

What were the vote numbers? Will the true count emerge?

Oh, yes. It is being conducted already.

Will there be a second vote?

That is not likely.

Will this be made "mainstream"?

Some, not all, but enough and eventually. **There is confusion for a while.** Not months, but the dust has to settle. **Things have been put in place and happen before then.** It will be made clear enough and **it will be a vastly different media by then.**

Is it cleaned up?

Not completely, **partially.** Enough so that facts emerge.

The public response demands it.

Enough so that the reasons for disruption are clear. Military presence is explained.

What follows are responses to questions concerning the virus/vaccine.

It is advised that you let that worry go. Focus on your new world and honest, clear contact.

It'll be June before that truth emerges. The focus changes before then, due to truths emerging about crimes against children, trafficking, etc.

There is quite a road before you now.

June before virus truths emerge?

June before it's beginning to be accepted as truth. A few major stories emerge that expose the connections and source of both the virus and the vaccine.

Your bodies have been altered. Massive amounts/doses are delivered to crystalline dominant bodies and have no subsequent effect one way or the other – harmful or helpful.

There is so much turmoil between now and June. There is a great

Words of One

deal of personal change forthcoming.

The facts are what change everything and they emerge by summer.

So, truth emerges this way?

- *1. Election*
- *1.(A) Money*
- *2. Trafficking children*
- *3. Virus/vaccine*

This is a good approximation, yes.

By what final date do we all have the facts? All of them?

It is seen that it completes itself by July.

July.

That is what is seen.

Not that it is over by then. But that it is known by then. Facts. Truth.

This next period of time is most difficult for you.

Things change, but there is some shock in store for all of you before it does. Then things change gradually. There is still some denial as a result of the shock.

This does work out with your relationships. In many cases you are and become closer because of this time.

It will be a most difficult time for you emotionally. It does end.

Thank you.

Words of One

February 23, 2021

It is the One.

Thank you.

I have questions.

Go ahead Sophia.

I seek information regarding timing, regarding relationships. I feel as if I have to let go of all that I know and love.

There are reasons to feel insecure. These make sense, in light of what happens now on your world. All, or many, of the things you expected to be there always, are dismantling, disintegrating before your eyes. This happens to things you haven't talked about much. This happens to things you discuss at great length.

What becomes a certainty is change – and that is not comforting. These times are times you "signed up for", before incarnating. You've always known, a part of you has always known anyway, that the world you'd grown accustomed to would collapse while you stood on her.

Even in the face of horrific slave-like conditions, you created for yourselves a sense of normalcy and regularity – a path to follow, that included expectations for achievements to reach at specific ages. You are not meant to suffer.

You will not suffer for long now. The anxiety you feel is present because of the unknown. It is present because of isolation. It is present due to the intentional insertion of fear and isolation into your population.

Your world will not collapse.

Your world is about to be re-born.

This feels awful right before it feels incredible. This feels never-ending for you now, yet I assure you, the end approaches.

The darkest moments that are immediately in front of you, all signal the end, the birth of the new.

You will not perish or collapse under the strain of this, but instead grow in strength. This happens as you get up day after day, and watch your world appear to be in a seeming state of collapse.

Remember that collapse occurs when there is no strength or ability to continue. Such is not the case. You were born for this moment.

It approaches.

Once revelations begin, you will notice an inner recognition, an "alarm" if you will, to alert you. This "alarm" is a reminder. You will not audibly hear it; you'll feel it internally.

What happens once you recognize it, is that as the revelations and changes continue, a part of you will approach them with calm assurance.

The end is near. The new is near. This is what carries you through with surplus strength, so that you are able to carry others.

Words of One

When and how and who?

There will not be another season of this anguish. Secrets are revealed to the masses before a fortnight. These have to do with such a deep level of corruption and global deception that they cannot be contained in a topic or single subject line or aspect of your society.

There is not so much a release of one truth after the other, in a specific and easily digested order.

No.

The deception is massive, global and complete. It will be exposed as that first.

Once it is comprehended that there has been a controlling element here, and that it essentially runs everything and has always done so – the dominos fall.

They fall rapidly and in order – a sequence that guarantees that all of the lies are exposed, all of the implications exposed.

It is not an easy process. It is, however, a complete one.

The old world is over, and in order for that fact to be accurately explained in a positive manner, the reasons for its necessary demise will have to be clear and obvious.

Truth is on its way.

Justice is part of the process.

Freedom follows the release of the old.

One of the important components to note as this transpires is that you as individuals do not have to release or lose each other in this process. What has to be released, however, is any method of relationship to either person, institution, or system that operated dishonestly or without agency.

You are entering a zero-point moment of authenticity.

You may be noticing self-realizations and internal discoveries that surprise you. Do not be alarmed by these noticing's and discoveries. You've been, until now, operating in a false construct, under rules of oppression and domination; however well-hidden they may have been.

You've had to wear many hats and many masks, in order to survive. As you see yourself without these, you may not recognize yourself. You will come to full recognition and self-authority. This will be a joyful state indeed.

You are meant to feel full without need of external validation. You are meant to operate with your complete personal power intact and functioning.

All this is before you now.

Remember.

Remember who you are.

Words of One

You are love.

You are light.

You are here to usher in a new world.

You will see, dear human, you will see. You will not be disappointed or anxious for much longer. You will be sustained and determined and reinforced once your shackles are clearly released.

You will see.

That is all.

Thank you.

Chapter 3. March

Words of One

It is the One.

You have reached the point of no return and are approaching your destination rapidly now. It is as if you speed downhill. There is one place that you are heading towards, and one place only. You head there as One.

It does not appear that way to the uninitiated. In fact, many of you who have taken this journey at other times, and in other places, do not remember having done so. This forgetting is intentional. It was agreed upon so that you would fully participate with each other…each moment of the journey discovered and subsequently felt – together. All to initiate further a sense of unity. All to accelerate Oneness.

For you are One, and you are realizing just what that means. There will not be a segment of the population who is left out of this unity, or who remain unaware. There will be One humanity, experiencing itself evolve and transform and become new. New in a sense of self-realized.

You've spent this lifetime uncovering how so much of what you'd imagined to be true, was actually defined by "other". Was actually a projection by "other". What you've accepted as truth, as necessary, as vital components to life, are in fact and in many cases, illusions perpetrated by the controllers here.

All of this becomes apparent now. This is what waits for you at the bottom of the hill that you are speeding down. Complete disclosure. Truth. Freedom from capture and a controlled reality. Controlled to a deeper and more sinister level than is currently acknowledged. This is completely made-up. None of it based on truth. All of it put in place to deceive in order to maintain dominance, perpetuate control and carry on doing so without a great deal of effort. In fact, to have it run this way on its own.

Systems and methods in place and orchestrated, by you[2], as unaware cogs in a great wheel of authority. This is going to be a real shock for so many. Now, it will not be an impossible to accept shock, but a surprise.

Acceptance will eventually be adopted, by everyone, as the truth of it becomes irrefutable. No place will you turn that will offer the illusion. The frequency has become such that the illusion cannot be sustained here. It is a bit like a tablet of color, dropped into a glass of water. It will not maintain its solid form and dissolves rapidly and inevitably and completely in that water. It is as if the tablet itself has disappeared. It has not, not completely. You will see remnants of it remain in the altered hue of the water. Yet, it is no longer together in solid form.

Your world has been intentionally fabricated in order to sustain and maintain a race and a culture that is not human, and therefore not motivated by human nature, but by its own. It has been this way always.

This race created culture and history that you've accepted as your own. What will be discovered as shocking and disturbing is that the "writing on the wall", that is now portrayed as ancient and removed from relevance in your modern world – **very much tells the story**

---

[2] *meaning humanity*

53

Words of One

of your beginning.

This beginning is not irrelevant — it is truth. What is needed now, in order for the story to make sense, is for the dots to be connected. There is a real lineage of rule and control and programming, that you, right now, display in your museums and texts of ancient history. Your DNA is becoming activated now so that remembering and connecting facts together is possible. It was not so easy to do that until now, although there have been whistle-blowers and truth-tellers always.

It's all connected.

It's all connected.

Those whistle-blowers came with a purpose. Their intent was to wake up the populace. They've been vilified and ignored and relegated to obscure bits of your history. Soon, they will be seen as the heroes they were. Their light was so powerful, that it blazed through the darkness of control here. So bright, that many of you know their names. Not a small feat.

The world today is filled with such light, and Gaia finds herself illuminated with truth. Truth blazes forth to rouse even the most fearful and reluctant. Realize it is fear that holds you in the darkness, and fear that you will have to release.

What you will experience upon learning and accepting as true, what is being done right now to your fellow humans and your children **is nothing compared to the life that they have led.** It is not up to you to feel bad or guilty about these horrors, although any feeling person will, **it is up to you to stop their continuing.**

This is done with light. The forces and groups and troops and teams who are infiltrating dens of human trafficking will be helped by your light, by your acceptance of what they do as necessary and valuable, by your holding firmly to the belief that it is evil and it must be stopped.

The only way forward is fearless.

The most powerful weapon now is love. This is an energetic battlefront, as well as a physical one.

Only some of you are among those actively engaged in removing and rescuing the children and trafficked humans. While **all of you contribute to the field of strength making that rescue possible.** Do you see?

There are members of your race without language or light, that right now remain collected and caged. Right now. As horrific as this all is, you've chosen to be here now, while it is being uncovered and disclosed, so that you could assist. The way to help is to believe. The way to help is to offer your strength, determination, and love to this process of liberation.

It happens first energetically. Any emotion other than love feeds those who would continue enslaving humanity. Fear does not assist; it only supports that which you are afraid of.

This next step asks you to believe what has been hidden beneath your feet, and to love. By love is meant accept. By love is meant support, not deny.

Words of One

From wherever you find yourself, you can offer your light. It is needed now.

It becomes for you now, and soon, an onslaught of disclosure, a downpour of truth. The scale of the deception has not been imagined. It will be massive and shocking.

It will **not** be your job to wake anyone up to the truth. No. You've been prepared in advance so that you can offer love, support and acceptance as others in your field hear, and accept as true, these things that you know. It is your job to love. It is your specialty actually, to love through the pain.

You will have no instruction manual, yet you won't and don't need one. Love is what you are and light is who you are. Truth is your calling card.

The goal now, for this next and upcoming part, is peace. Your light and love will emit a sense of calm in a tumultuous moment. It serves as a beacon and draws those near, offering direction.

Do not worry about finding those who need your help. You have placed yourself there and are, right now, precisely where you meant to be and are most needed.

Remember that all that you are learning about, everything being disclosed **has already happened.** Realize that the best use of your power is to focus on **what happens next.**

It is time to use your creative ability, your visualization, your light, your love – to build tomorrow.

What gets stronger, does so with frequent use. Now is the time to love relentlessly. Now is the time for continuous light.

None of what is to come will be easy, yet none of it is too much for you to see. It is **precisely** what you came to carry, as well as your brothers and sisters in need of a lift.

The force of your light will draw others to you within range. It is why you find yourselves scattered all over the globe. You are right where you decided to be for this coming moment.

You are about to realize your gifts and abilities. You are about to contribute to disclosure and the awakening of the race.

We will speak again soon.

That is all.

Thank you.

Words of One

It is the One.

Circumstances remain the same, and thus escalate. The reasons for this are many, while at the forefront are the conflicting explanations, interpretations and responses. All of this intentional. All of this directed psychological weaponry.

For if you can't convince all of the herd to go in the direction you desire, you can instead confuse them so that they end up going in circles. This, at the very least, prevents all of them from going in the opposite direction to which you desire.

The mental anguish and confusion among so many, has increased over time, not decreased. There will be a reckoning, which for that moment will bring everyone together. This will be followed by a choosing. It will not be easy, while the choice will be straight forward. The options available to select will be hand-picked. Divine intervention assures this.

For many of you, "divine intervention" are words with little relevance and no substantive definition. What does that look like? What does it mean?

It means an installation of an event that is not, nor could it ever be, man-made. This fact will be evident to all when it takes place. This fact will be the one obvious truth.

When divine intervention occurs, many questions are answered. When divine intervention occurs, all of humanity is on the same page.

This is a planned event. This will happen. Trust.

No more specifics will be given here.

When it occurs, there will be no questions. It will supply you with answers.

That is all.

Thank you.

Goodbye Sophia, my chosen one.

Words of One

It is the One.

Nothing but your/the Ascension takes precedence now. For all of
your aspects, every one of your timelines and "dimensions". All
eyes, hearts and energetic impulses are focused right here, right
now, on this very moment which you are creating now. This life.
Your life in 2021.

For this is the most glorious culmination of collective love, an
outpouring of generational, universal intent – a brilliant force of
cosmic light.

This moment is unique. The build-up to its eventual completion is
something not before seen. For the Dark have done their part, and
so completely, and in such a spectacular display of stubborn refusal
to submit, that **this time** is unlike **any other** in dramatic
expression, violent display, and absolute breathtaking conviction of
role. Each pair of shoes firmly embedded in their chosen spot in
the sand. The reveal is poised to be spectacular.

For this is a performance really. While it continues, you are focused
on good guys and bad guys, rescues and heroes, hurts and
triumphs, sinners and saints. At its completion, the masks and
costumes come off. The real source and identity of each player in
full reveal.

You are not dealing with only humans, but mostly humans. There
are identities that will surprise you. There is still, and at this late
date, actors and roles and reveals that will shock you. "Shock"

meaning that you'll find them to be completely unexpected.

For this has been the most magnificent performance, conducted by Masters. These Masters surround you now. It will ask you to look around today and see that. It will ask you to look beyond the mask.

One of the more challenging and even difficult components of full awareness will soon be apparent. It all gets swept up in Oneness. It is then that, while still playing the part, the human role you embody now, you will look around and realize that those you have hated, vilified, honored and praised, are absolutely cut from One cloth. They spring from One Source. It is the same Source you are. You are One.

Once you are able to take the perspective of willing participant rather than victim, you will begin to realize the full range of your being.

These are words that perhaps sound hollow to your human ears. You live right now in a world gone mad, and as part of an oppressed slave race. Yes, this is your current role.

It is not your only role, nor has it been always on the side of the light. You have participated at every level and all sides.

As a Master, you have committed yourself to excellence.

The exquisite result of your efforts waits for you right now. It peeks around the corner, its brilliance unable to be contained or diminished by the Dark.

For you **are** the Masters of the Universe, putting on right now a magnificent performance for us all. For us all, as One.

You volunteered for this final act and were chosen for this final act. It is the "Superbowl" of Ascension Events and its players are in top form and ready.

Imagine the store of energy that builds for this culmination. Thousands of years of oppression and frustration and suppression. The Massive Force of your emotions thus propel this Ascension Event.

Do you see?

Do you see why this moment, **even this moment,** is created by you?

It has always been you.

The pain, the glory and the decision to finally bring it to a close is all yours.

Dear, dear precious human. This life in shackles that you are seeing and breaking out of now, is merely one of many, many, many experiences. Experiences you've completed to gain perspective, and to perfect love. Throughout them all, you've built muscle and honed technique, delving deep into each nuance possible.

All so that you would know, without separation, what it is to be alive.

You've played your roles with gusto and still do today. As immersion feeds you with knowledge and sensitivity.

You are Masters, perfecting your craft.

You are here to create worlds.

That is all.

Thank you.

Note:
So much came through with this! Huge download of visuals and emotions. Seeing all of us as Masters, orchestrating both sides, like puppet "Masters" almost, without strings.

Saw from Ancient to Modern times, a collective build-up of horror and pain and what that builds to, the power of that, the force of that, the brilliance of that. Words aren't enough to encapsulate the accumulation and its intent.

I saw generations, civilizations, angels, multiple races, ancestors and brethren from the stars — all watching, smiling, together and right here with us. A "we've got your back" cushion of absolute pure love. Magnificent doesn't do it justice. We are not alone. Not by a longshot.

What happens next is fueled by every lifetime, every role; by the All that is. It's epic.

Sophia

Words of One

March 8th, 2021
3:45 AM

It is the One.

There are things to say. These things concern your liberty. These things concern your well-being, your health, your life as a human being in this year of 2021.

For it is all set to change, about to be altered, and in some ways, unrecognizable from that which you have known thus far.

You have never been free. Not in recent memory. Not truly.

You've experienced the appearance of freedom within a very structured existence, operating within somewhat invisible walls. These walls put in place by society, by governments, by invisible rulers pulling unseen strings.

The subtle shift from invisible control into visible, actual visceral restraint and programming with masks, lockdowns and injections was only possible because of that initial and invisible control already in place.

What is shocking and abhorrent to the portion of the population who are awake now, does not feel that different actually, to those who are still drowsy. The voice of authority, granting rules and permissions and instructions, is one they do not regard as evil or manipulative, but instead comforting and necessary.

It will not be until the truth is made clear, apparent and unquestionable, that this changes for them. The source of this information will come from, indeed must come from, an authority who is deeply trusted.

This will not be a fellow human with a "different opinion", but from a voice holding power and weight. Someone they naturally trust.

The cage of bars is every bit as real, now, as ever. It is about to be not only unlocked, but dissolved. What remains, once it is gone, is self-authority.

The idea of true liberty bears with it, great responsibility. It is not a "get out of jail free" card. It is a statement of authentic self-rule.

What is occurring, and right now, is the human version of the elephant story. This story we've spoken of before. It is worth mentioning that she wraps that chain around her own leg willingly, and without thought, not because she is impaired in some way. She is quite intelligent. She believes and therefore desires what she considers to be normal and necessary. She has not yet experienced life without the weight of the chain, and does not desire to.

It's not an option for her, because she's never considered or seen it. It's not actually real for her. Without the chain, she cannot rest, and therefore she replaces it herself when the trainer forgets. She has a peaceful night's sleep once she does.

This partially explains what happens now, on earth, with the split in the human race. It explains why it is possible to introduce tighter restrictions, and more invasive (to some) sounding actions and have them met with compliance and even insistence that they happen. The race wants relief from this terrifying disease that's been inflicted upon them. For many, relief can only show up in the hands of some outside **and more powerful** voice of authority. From someone trusted, someone who has a vested interest in their well-being.

This divide in the race is not because one side wants different outcomes than another side. It is because one side believes that the path to those outcomes must include adherence to recommended methods given by specific and very authoritative voices. While another side has come to trust other voices and messages, an internally spoken authority that replaces the current mouthpiece and resonates in a deeper way.

These are not new voices, yet they've grown louder and more insistent now and are drowning out the more prominent mouthpieces.

The frequency supports and encourages internal authority as well as propels it. This frequency shift increases its vibration, and the pressure that is expelled as it does so, changes hearts and minds. "Change" is the operative word here. For it must be remembered that for each of you, the options and decisions will differ, and they cannot be laid out by another as more or less "correct".

The decision as to which choice is highest and best is an individual one. It will be made that way. These incoming frequencies demand that and allow that.

Where this conversation began, is about the concept of true liberty. This truth will not be something that can be stopped. Herein lies the secret. It is why your oppressors always and ultimately fail at total control. It is not possible for one soul to completely own another. It will never be possible.

There is a great deal of posturing and play and appearance of ownership. There is surface evidence for slavery and it is compelling. Yet, it is not complete, and not possible. It is a powerful illusion, intentionally operated, to convince you of its reality.

Why does JFK Jr. keep going through my head?

Because you see him as a potential voice of authority. You are seeing pieces fit into this puzzle, and you wonder how or who could pull off such a switch, as to mesmerize and reveal truth to the sleeping and drowsy ones. JFK Jr. seems to be the right candidate for this, does he not?

I tell you this – you are poised now to witness a massive turnaround and upheaval in society, authority and information. This upsets what has been seen as trustworthy, and puts something new in its place.

Inquiry. Wonder. A belief in the miraculous. A resurgence of faith in the goodness of people.

These revelations come coupled with horror, as truths are exposed around the depths of depravity and destruction taking place under the control of those who've held the reins until now. It is a costly realization.

Yet, not unlike the birth of a child with accompanying labor pains, a worthy one. One worth doing. Once it occurs, one you could not imagine going forward without.

Words of One

Liberty will be understood once the chains are seen. Once seen, they dissolve and there is a feeling of "unbound" that accompanies their dissolution.

Liberty will be the initial term for what happens next. As indeed you are being liberated from a constructed reality that hindered your sight.

Freedom comes next, and it is a heady term. There will be many crashes as none of you are used to the speeds at which you can fly. Your wings have been clipped until now. You will not succumb because of these crashes, but will learn from them. You will help each other and learn together the possibilities and nuances of freedom. Limitless is not a term you've understood. You will discover it next.

So much of your life and history has been held in chains that it will feel confusing for you and look chaotic.

Imagine[3] a room full of toddlers, wall to wall, all attempting to take their first few steps at the same time. There will be bumps, bruises and crashes a-plenty. Yet, the internal motivation to walk will force the process for them all, and they will not stop, not ever, until they

---

[3] *Visual here was wonderful. There was a room the size of a barn with these toddlers, and they were each filled with determination as they crashed and fell and got up. No angry faces or cries of pity or helplessness, these were tenacious little people, with huge smiles, just thrilled to be taking their first steps. What began as a mess, eventually became cooperative movement. It was astounding and powerful and simply, beautifully illustrative of our next phase! It was a thrill to witness as well as experience.*

can run. And they will figure out how to do so without crashing into one another. It will become, eventually and beautifully, an orchestrated movement filled with joy and the rush of adrenaline as they now can move, on their own, upright and strong.

This room of crashing toddlers eventually morphs into a sea of smiling angels – moving effortlessly around each other, with each other, and in perfect synchronicity.

This is where you go, dear human. This is where you are heading. This is the realization of true freedom, and this is the experience of achieving liberty.

You are about to witness a miracle.

You are about to achieve such heights and depths of your being that the brief chaos introducing this moment will be all but forgotten in its glory.

Hang on to your hats, while you let go your grip on all that you knew to be real. You'll want your hands in the air for this part of the ride. No worries, for you can fly.

You are in for such a treat.

That is all.

Thank you.

Goodbye Sophia, my chosen one.

Words of One

March 11, 2021

It is the One.

Thank you. I have some questions.

Go ahead, Sophia.

Thank you. A fortnight has passed. Would you say what it was that you were referring to?

There are more truths revealed, yet not the supremely conclusive totality of the situation here. What was referred to two weeks past was the accumulation. The partial indicators are seen by anyone paying attention. The focus is on England; the royal family, the bank of England. Also, there are other financial indicators. It will come out in odd and various places for some time. It has to.

The world of humanity is in many ways so very drowsy. What are needed are cracks in the currently held belief system/the currently held reality. The actions by the current and falsely won presidency are giving many in your country food for thought and reasons to wonder. This election fakery will be the first domino to fall. It will fall. There will be unrest when it does.

The sum total of truth to be disclosed is massive in number. It covers many areas of life and people will find themselves in desperate confusion.

What has been said, and repeatedly, holds true. The genie behind the curtain is made known as reality initially. The story. All in its right timing.

You enter a tumultuous time because of these outings and truths, these cracks in the foundation of reality. It is moving along in such a way so that the highest and best outcome is reached, and the largest numbers of humans are reached.

There are no mistakes. There are many players orchestrating the show. Everyone with their lines, some waiting in the que.

There are things that have to happen so that people have every opportunity to wake up.

They are synchronized. This is a fluid situation.

I was interrupted here and had to stop unexpectedly.

Words of One

March 16, 2021
3:22 AM

What happens here on earth is this — the layers of involvement and methods of participation vary so extremely and vastly that they do not even see each other... All of the players here for the same game.

For while this is not meant to downplay or disregard the crimes against humanity still occurring, it is meant to step way back to answer the questions of "why?" and "when?".

It is a deep challenge for you at times to step back from this daily life and look at the whole. Yet, there is where you will find solace and so there is where your answers, truthful answers, are found.

You are multi-dimensional, many aspects simultaneously occurring. This now moment repeated for other versions of you at other "times" — yet in an instant.

This means that currently, your deep dive into the truth about life and manipulation on earth in 2021, happens at the same time that the broader part of you with a greater vision into the purpose of it all occurs.

Wisdom. Depth of purpose. Clarity. All of these, aspects of Ascension.

Remember, that this is not only about you (*lower case/ small/ individual*) — it is also about **YOU** *(upper case/ collective/ broad)* — all of **you as One.**

Regardless of your like or dislike for any personality, any human here on earth and right now – **you are all here for the same purpose.**

I speak here of humans. The race that initiated and perpetrated the enslavement is another category.

You ask why it continues still and now.

I tell you this. It will continue until the world agrees that it stop.

There are sequences of events that forecast that, and once they begin, the dominoes rapidly fall.

All of the prior predictions remain. This is a fluid situation. Focus and intent are necessary components now, and will have to be utilized incessantly. This is a frequency battle.

You are being helped enormously with energy shifts, while maintenance of the highest vibrations is up to the human population.

What slows this down?

Almost nothing can, at this point, and for certain it will not be able to be stopped. Yet, arguments, divisiveness, blame, polarization. All of these are time wasters and distracters.

This is a battle, **the final battle.**

Unlike most video game's final battles, there is no **final boss.** No.

Words of One

There is a mass of desperate members of the "evil" side, scrambling at illusions of power, grasping at straws of control, attempting to stand their ground.

They will have to be forced out – they will not surrender or leave on their own.

There is no delay. There is divine timing. Those of you, all of you, participating perfectly in the exact method you agreed to.

What will help is further emanations of love.

What will help is an expansion of light.

In every direction, to every dark corner and each dark player.

Even those you despise.

There is only one way to finish this, and that is by playing the final card.

It has not been played.

You will see, dear human, you will see.

That is all.

Thank you.

Goodbye Sophia, my scribe, my chosen one.

Words of One

It is the One.

You have reached a stage in your development which brings you face to face with your origins, your roots, your originators. Here is where all things began and here you will find truth. Answers to questions only guessed at. Absolute discovery and uncovering of all that has been hidden.

The time before you will be revelatory, in ways previously unimagined. There has never been an uncovering as the one you are close to witnessing.

All truths revealed. All identities disclosed. You will not come through this time without surprises. In some cases, shocks. For the programming has been deep, prolonged and relentless. It is the way of this race, and well honed. (this non-human race)

The fact of its end, is not one factored in, ever. What has been seen by your controllers is perpetual control. This idea, now transferred to the human components on earth, creates for you a vicious final battle. Every illusory trick and weaponized system are in play now. They will not release their grip.

Yet, and here, dear human, is the news that you can rely on as truth. This time now with its frequency and accelerated light — trumps every card they hold. There is no ending that sees them in control.

You have done it. The race (the human race) has won. Due to the nature of reality on this third dimensional earth, it does not appear to be so today.

The children. The tunnels. What about the trafficking?

Right now, operations are in play to completely sweep them clean. This is a dirty business Sophia, and utmost care must be taken so that maximum lives are saved.

There are some operations still active, yes. They are known and targeted. There has to be secrecy and the element of surprise. The delicacy of these operations cannot be over-stated.

Once the "all-clear" is given, it will mean that the children are safe. This is your divine timing and will result in a divine intervention before it is finished.

The breadth and depth and scope of these rescue operations cannot be over-stated. If there is anything more massive, it would be the healing for them all – emotional, physical, spiritual, mental. You will have help there with technology, yet this will consume mankind for some time. Heal, repair, renew. This will be your future.

You will claim this victory full-on and proceed to formulate a new era. This one based on freedom, on sovereignty, on love, on light. You will see, dear human, you will see.

That is all.

Words of One

Thank you.

March 22, 2021
5:50 AM

It is the One.

Things occur now that are worthy of discussion here. These are subjects not normally on a daily conversation list, yet they apply to what occurs on your planet, and for you now.

They are methods of life, ways of approaching what you may consider sacred, or not. Things that are wrapped up in your society and labeled this way or that due to beliefs and to those things handed down to you from generations. These are many. These are varied. These cause disruptions in Oneness.

For you see large groups who schedule prayer and devotion and genuflection several times in their day. Then you see others who have no such custom of scheduled prayer.

Your knowledge is limited, Sophia, regarding religious practices and cultural norms. So, this discussion will appear to be on the surface only. It, however, applies to each differing cultural expression regarding some sort of God.

You do not often think about other forms of devotion, worship or prayer than your own. Yet each moment they are conducted by humans across the globe. These humans are identical to you in heart and passion and capacity for love. These humans express themselves differently yet are no different.

At the end of every day, humans hold a belief in something greater than themselves.

Words of One

All creatures do not. All sentient, intelligent creatures who live in societies do not. The reference here is to not only other species, but other worlds.

For there are humans everywhere.

What will help you to understand the whole, is that these different methods of worship, these ideas of something greater than themselves, are ideas that were introduced, taught and fostered in the race here. All of them hold origins that propel one race to grandeur and another "lesser" race to servitude of some sort.

This is not to label religious practice as wrong or to lump all of its teachings into a basket of manipulation.

It is to illustrate that among sovereign beings – worship does not exist.

This truth illustrates an idea so comprehensive and inclusive, that it becomes difficult to comprehend in your daily life.

For is not all life sacred?

Is not there a creator of all life?

Is not the intelligence fueling that life a single unifying consciousness?

The answer is yes.

The lifeblood of universal awareness does not require specifics in order to be pleased. It merely is. It exists in a balanced state; defining, describing and plotting universal movement according to its driving force – discovery and more life.

If there is a sentiment to describe this universal intelligence, it would be:
"Yes please, <u>more</u>!"

It knows only expansion.

There are multitudes of possible expressions of life, all equally valid, honored and necessary.

As humanity makes its way across the vast stream of possibilities for itself, it must place rocks to stand on along the route. Each stone a marker, a point of reference.

The stone may be an idea, a cultural realization, a set of rules, even a person. None of these are wrong. All of these are temporary.

The stones used for passage across the moving stream of life are not meant to take permanent residence on. They are markers and guides, places that lead you to, or make possible, other places.

You will not be able to see certain and necessary stones until you reach certain and necessary other stones.

It is a journey.

This trip you take now leads to Oneness. The fullness of Unity allows for freedom of thought and practice without necessitating control and uniformity.

Words of One

Oneness is not sameness. Unity implies a single connecting facet that is undeniable. In this case, the case of which we speak, humanity, this facet is light.

There is but one light.

Sections of it have been hidden in darkness, camouflaged by deceit.

There is but one love.

Whole portions of it seem to have been "lost" at times. Yet it was merely suppressed then. Suppressed by fear.

Sovereignty obliterates weakness. There is no "need" to be "right" or to prove oneself once sovereignty exists.

Dialogue and discussion are part of the journey. You live in a mirrored existence. How will you see truth until and unless it is reflected back to you?

This is the reason for humanity at all.

This is what the process calls for. A constant show of possibilities. The truth will expose itself in your fulfillment once realized.

You will not "require" anything once that occurs. You will merely and absolutely **know.**

The methods to get there are as varied as grains of sand. Together, a beach. Yet able to be individually moved and identified.

All paths lead to Oneness. For Oneness is truth and the underlying principle of life itself. All grains necessary, yet some more pivotally placed. The whole is not possible without each element contributing its part.

The One is not to be worshipped. Yet it is to be considered, recognized and held sacred.

Reverence for the One implies the sacred nature of every component. Life can be understood through this statement.

There are forces being exposed now that actively pursue destruction of that reverence and promote an opposite and abhorrent idea.

These are specific, and directed efforts to accomplish certain and destructive ends. It becomes important in these coming days of disclosure, exposure and re-structuring, that humanity refrain from labeling every alternative pattern or form "depraved". Not all of it is.

Discernment, always discernment.

You may not like or agree with specific practices. Yet God, the One, has no such thought.

That is all.

Thank you.

Words of One

Goodbye, Sophia, my chosen one.

March 24, 2021
3:31 AM

It is the One.

You are right now looking at your final days. It is not meant that you are about to die. It is meant that your known civilization is on the cusp of such massive upheaval as to be unrecognizable.

I speak now of more the immediate future than is typically discussed. I speak now of the coming months.

For the only way to upend and uproot and remove the coils of control holding humanity in its grip is to do so drastically, suddenly and absolutely finally.

There are deals that have been struck. There are arrangements which have been made. This game has many players and they orchestrate many parts.

It's as if you will be surprised at every turn. It's as if it has all been a lie.

Not only the guise of "freedom" held so closely to society's machinations, but also to the exposure of truth.

All of it is orchestrated.

The take down must be complete. There can be no re-occurrence of pseudo-benefactors for humanity.

The only thing holding up now is truth.

Words of One

Truth.

The idea so intrinsic to autonomy yet so beyond reach in this current and crumbling matrix as to be unrecognizable.

Confusion reigns and this is only the beginning.

The parts, roles and players of both will be shocking, devastating, and revelatory once announced. Announcements are forthcoming.

What you can be sure of is the inevitability of the light. It holds its place now, and only expands, illuminating all dark corners and hidden agendas.

This is not the place in which names are given. This is the place that offers substance and background to what human life has become, and what the race is accomplishing now.

This is the place to remind you, dear star seed, of the reason you came at all.

For your part in this drama has not always been as clear and direct as it is now. There have been lives and parts murkier, darker. There have been roles, and many, in which what occurred was an exploration of limits. These have included control, degradation pain and horror. All elements of human action are parts of the human experience. All components of ego explored.

For what is ego?

A participatory agenda taken on in order to explore extreme

possibilities of human addiction and response. A necessary cloak, worn on the way to Ascension and eventually shed.

The possibility to adopt a new facet, a novel ego, is forever present.

There is no right or wrong, good or bad, up or down. All is metaphor and illustration, useful in the explanation of an illusory existence. It's played out in such a way so that polarization explains it, illustrates the obvious.

Obvious only once another perspective is reached. Not clear while in the trenches, while immersed in ego, dripping in right and wrong, godly and sinner, good and bad.

Every part necessary. All players on equal footing.

Judgment has no place in evolution.

It's all allowed in a state of balance.

Those of you who've found each other now and are particularly invested in promoting the awakening have all participated in other, darker and more self-motivated roles.

Other "times".

There is no judgment. There is only love. It lives in light and propels evolution.

These words are not irrelevant. These are the fullness of the arch of life, the blueprint for mankind, the evolution and the awakening of this chosen race.

Words of One

Humanity represents all things and every possibility. It is in the depths of despair and the recesses of self-absorption where self is discovered
.

An awakened human is a formidable foe, an unstoppable force, a pure source of love and a brilliant light.

This is the reason for the powerful and brilliant plan to keep you held in captivity.

It's been said before, yet worth mentioning here that it had to be executed gradually, like the frog in a pot of water that slowly raises its temperature. There have been generations of adjustments, all accepted, before the heat was obvious.

It's obvious now. This is part of the plan. Those who notice will have every opportunity to jump out before succumbing.

Realize that the seers are seeing possibilities. These are not the same as probabilities. They are warnings.

There is not an ending in which the race succumbs to control.

There is only one end, and it includes the Ascension of the Race of Man.

That is all.

Thank you.

Goodbye my chosen one, my scribe.

Words of One

March 26, 2021
3:30 AM

It is the One.

We have a few topics which have yet to be addressed. These concern military operations, and also, points of order. Both are factions of this constructed society which provide a sense of control and comfort to the citizenry of most countries. This, of course, saying "most", because in a small number of countries the military has been used as a weapon against the people, and not as a force of protection **for** the people. It has become, in these cases, a "captured" operation, used by the controllers.

Spotting either individuals, institutions, or portions of government that are "captured" becomes an easy thing once you understand what to look for. Any such faction will demonstrate loyalties with actions, not words. There are not hidden meanings in much of what is said. There are blatant lies at this point, and obvious loyalties.

It is in the actions of such perpetrators where the truth of motivation is revealed.

Government has become, in the majority of cases, a "captured" enterprise. While this is not the case with the military, and that is worth remembering.

When you witness military control specifically, you are going to have to observe carefully to discern whether or not this is protection from or oppression by the controllers in said country.

Things to look for are these:

> Past actions by current military leaders.
> Attitudes and actions towards an armed citizenry.
> Loyalties – who do their actions benefit ultimately?
> Use of force presented.
> The care & comfort & feeding of these forces.

While military forces are designed to obey their superior offices, there is a deeper oath. That oath is protection of the people. Any forces turned against their own populace have become weapons and are thus "captured".

The discussion here is being held now because you are seeing conflict within your government, as well as your military officials. This conflict will eventually reach a boiling point, and it will help to know that all is not lost when that happens. It is a sorting.

There are layers of players. While it may appear obvious as to who is on what "side", it becomes important in this final act of the performance not to make assumptions.

There are some players who act for one or the other "side", while pretending not to.

We've spoken of this before. Things are about to get very confusing. Some are unwittingly serving the opposite "side". While most, at this late date, are clear in their motivation.

When you witness military control and action within any country – pay attention to precise details of the actions taken.

Words of One

Who is served?
How is the movement orchestrated?
Who are the "enemies" as adopted by the actions taken?

Remember that the military does not serve itself in any case. It exists as an arm of those generals and officials in control. It is the aim of those generals and officials that needs to be scrutinized in order to determine just who is being served.

Ultimately, it becomes necessary to examine its leadership.

While in the recent past, this may have not been easily accomplished – things are in the final moments now and evidence more obvious.

You will have to remain awake and aware during these upcoming days.

Do not fall into fear when the military enters the scene. It can be said that in the majority of cases, this will be an indication that the players you've named the "white hats" have moved into place for the finale.

As in any good show, there are twists and turns and surprises. All of these adding excitement as well as confusion.

It becomes important to remember that the controlling force of the planet specializes in military tactics. It was always going to come to this.

You will want to hold faith in the idea that there is no possible scenario in which the controllers retain control. None.

These final shows of force will be clumsy at best, catastrophic at worst. All timelines end with light.

It comes from multiple sources, the military included.

This is an attempted hostile takeover and thus there will be some hostilities before it is complete. Stories have to play out. The timeline will reach its conclusion naturally, and through human action.

There is a convergence of timelines at the final stages. You approach such a moment.

These coming times will require faith and discernment and the ability to adapt as players remove their masks and true motivations are revealed. Trust the process.

Shine always the light that emanates from your heart.

You are witnessing the birth of a new world.

That is all.

Thank you.

Goodbye Sophia, my chosen one.

Words of One

March 30, 2021
4:42 AM

It is the One.

There are subjects to consider.

Your way of life has been altered. It is about to be, once more, changed. The changes this time will feel gradual and although unusual, as in different, more comfortable. They will become common place and permanent to a greater extent than what occurs for you now. They follow a natural order and are easily adapted to.

This is a reference to self-rule. It concerns a basic tenet of your society, and the subject of sovereignty.

For what has occurred for the race is a change-over and a take-over of its natural cooperative tendency, into one both more war-like as well as more obedient and power hungry.

Although the extremes seem opposite (*power hungry vs obedient)*, they are, in fact, the core nature of the race which now attempts complete control of the humans here – the reptilian race.

They have not succeeded and will not succeed. Not in a take-over, and not completely.

What has been accomplished, instead, is a gradual infiltration into the race of the tendency to obey authority regardless of outcome, the desire for power-over, and ownership. These personality components are prized in power-hungry arenas and seen as elements of dominance to be almost worshipped.

Let us speak now of the human in his/her natural state, before the reptilian influence.

This race is a peaceful one. It is hybrid to its core, and encompasses a great many traits that create diversity, flexibility and tolerance.

The human on earth is known for brilliance, ingenuity, compassion, loyalty and love. Their dedication to the whole is one of their most prominent traits.

The earth humans are prized and revered. Their strength and capacity for endurance makes a powerful combination. Yet, at their core, they do not seek power-over, but instead power-with. This is a communal race, who take the most joy in union, in celebrations together, in community and in common purpose.

The removal and complete eradication of the dominant reptilian energy from the race will open the door to a new day for the race. New avenues of society will be seen as possible and thus followed.

Things leaving will be…

Mockery for being "different".

Labels of "weakness" that surround those less obviously forceful, and therefore   more peace loving.

A desire for complete control.

Words of One

Things re-introduced will be...

    Celebration of alternative views and opinions.

    Collaboration as antidote, rather than confrontation.

    Autonomy rather than obedience.

    Self-authority.

What will be the most appreciated and felt will be the idea of Unity. Oneness will be experienced viscerally, as humanity's true nature is free to be expressed.

Evidence of its expression will be primarily evident in systems of rule, governance, and societal control.

The idea of "rule for thee and not me" will not be a part of things.

Instead, those who have more to do with the machinations of society will naturally consider the whole and bring it into the decision-making process. The environment, equality in food distribution and wealth, education and healing modalities will be prominent here. These, rather than greed, ownership, dominance and lust.

These changes are possible as the planet moves to another frequency and leaves these darker more controlling elements completely. These changes will not emerge through force, but instead through natural cohesion and innate power.

The human is a gem. A powerful, beautiful instance of creation that has been manipulated and thus hidden because of it. Not completely hidden, no. The brilliance and unique nature of the human has carried the race to its current place. You stand on the doorstep of a magnificent transformation.

Your evolution will be one for the history books, **is** one for the history books, and now witnessed by all of Creation.

Humanity demonstrates what is possible when freedom of choice is held as a core principle. There are things that have not ever been stifled, not completely. These make up the drive for true freedom and the push for equality.

What emerges now is nothing more than your original blueprint. The makers signature has not been erased through all these eons of suppression and conflict. It's merely been obscured and forgotten.

Not any longer.

You are about to realize the fullness of your potential. Hue-man 2.0 emerges amid the ashes of disguise and the wreckage of control.

You cannot halt the process of Mastery. You can only feed it, with discovery of unknown abilities through adaptation and development. At its core, at **your** core, is truth, love and light. Nothing in all of Creation conquers that.

Self-awareness naturally evolves into emergence, and the society solves for itself any non-cooperative dilemmas. You will be astounded at the base simplicity of Oneness. Once implemented and accepted, it answers all questions and diminishes conflict.

Words of One

These are eventual outcomes of the process now inhabited by the race. What is witnessed now is the 3D shattering of all that is false.

Truth, love and light, offer the only solid response and become your "go to" arenas. As a result, society will appear to engage in an upheaval. This is necessary and short-lived. It becomes important to stay clear of fear, as this lengthens the process.

Your natural tendency towards collaboration will arise once fear abates. It is a gorgeous uprising indeed.

You will see, dear human, you will see

That is all.

Thank you.

Goodbye Sophia, my chosen one.

Chapter 4. April

Words of One

It is the One.

Not only are you about to witness the miraculous, but you are about to simultaneously experience the miraculous. Together, as a single organism. Individually, in your unique fashion.

What approaches next in your Ascension journey is a bit of a ride. It is one that you've not taken before. Not while in form and not in conjunction with the planetary body on which you rest. There are not adequate descriptions to describe this. You will be inventing them once it is complete.

What may be helpful now is to discuss the fear element. Fear of the unknown. Fear of the new. Fear of change. These three elements – unknown, new and change – do not necessitate fear. They will be more successfully and satisfactorily met with anticipation.

The resulting world on which you will find yourself will be one of peace, harmonious interaction, receptivity and growth. These are attributes to be celebrated and you will, more than likely, quickly adjust. Just wait until you see your new world.

It will help you to navigate this moment with a sense of joy. Imagine a child in the days and weeks before Christmas. Regardless of what is happening at each moment, he or she remains in a good mood because of what is about to happen. Sometimes it is almost too much, and emotions get out of hand. Yet always there remains a knowing that in a matter of days – good things are coming.

This will be more than Christmas morning for you. This will be waking up to every aspect of life upgraded.

Try to envision a sense of strength physically, purpose mentally, peace spiritually and bliss emotionally. There is a vibrancy, an aliveness and drive that accompanies the frequency shift you are undertaking. Everything will experience a sense of internal direction that is self-driven, rather than manipulated from someplace or someone else.

It makes sense that your bodies are reacting now, as well as the rest of you. As a whole, you are experiencing the shift. It is both gradual and sudden.

There is no way to declare the precise 3D moment in which it will occur. **This will happen when all of you decide. This will happen in the perfect moment and according to divine timing.**

What also may help is the knowing that there is not one person or one source that ultimately determines the "timing". That source you seek or expect exists within the whole itself. It does not stand outside of the whole. **It is the whole.**

Although you may perceive what you call "divine intervention", this too will depend on point of view and will occur in concert with the choice of the whole.

All sides work together for this Ascension. There is a reality beneath the headlines, where all of you are following the same script and knowing the final act. It is that reality which drives your life as played out now.

Words of One

The extreme focus on division, separation, good guys or bad guys is part of the show. There are some excellent and experienced actors for this show. It creates a mesmerizing and convincing performance.

What you'll find shocking perhaps will be the lies that have been told. These include some major and world changing events. There is no way to prepare for these. Their uncovering will expose the depths of this matrix of control in a way that would not otherwise be believed.

What becomes more productive than anything else now, is a sense of unity. Oneness is the end result of this shift as all facets of it only accelerate the process.

What happens individually for you all now is a definition of oneness, but personally.

There will be situations in your life that bring forth the necessity to see a loved one or at least a very close one in a new light. This will occur, somehow, for each of you.

Know that your interactions now, housemates now, situations now, and location now have been specifically chosen for this time. You are meant to be right where you are, with exactly who you are, for the coming shift. "Meant" to be, not because an outside force or source decided it was so, but because you did.

You will experience this shift, have chosen to experience this shift, in the most optimal fashion possible. This means that you'll achieve the greatest benefit from it. You chose and were chosen to be here for this. It is an honor and a massive undertaking for you to be. This will yield both intense participation and unequalled joy.

Some will call it a "reward", and in a sense the word fits. It is an earned result and you'll know the effort necessary intimately. You know it now.

This evolution and Ascension are both happening now, and before you now.

It is not something to wait for. It is something to do.

There is a state of mind that will speed up the process and it includes assistance, unity, awareness and acceptance. **Oneness is inevitable and true. It already exists.**

What you are actually doing is waking up to that fact. In this sense, even the more spiritually "enlightened" among you have yet to grasp it in fullness.

As has been said before — all of you are in for a surprise. It is called "The Great Awakening" with good reason. No one is left behind and there are truths beneath the fabric of your current reality that assure this is so.

In whatever way possible to muster, conjure unity in your days. The broadcasting of that singular frequency will permeate the whole, and organically move you closer to the finish line.

It will be reached when you all get there together, and not a moment before.

Words of One

You will see, dear human, you will see.

That is all.

Thank you.

April 3, 2021
3:30 AM

It is the One.

There are things to say.

These concern money and the system of debt in which you live under. These are the weapons of control utilized here by the ones who consider themselves owners; owners of humanity.

Money and Debt Systems are fairly brilliant in doing precisely what it is they were built for. That is, building worlds held together by invisible slavery.

You are about to experience the opposite of all that you've ever known. For an un-slaved race holds no concept of "owe" or "debt" or "rich" or "poor". These attributes are only possible when money exudes its brute force and runs the show.

It is difficult for you to imagine a world without the underlying voice of money, but for a moment let us try.

There are some basic ideas that would not be a part of such a world. They include:

Poverty
Greed
Market manipulation and control
Needing a "job"
Homelessness
Neglected health (or any basic need) due to cost

Words of One

The 1 %
Tax
Banks
Banking
Starvation
Monopolies
Upper/lower "classes"

These are just a few. The entire structure of society will crumble, leaving room for something new.

This "new" will have to be created, imagined by the hue-man 2.0, and allow for things like:

Free
Equality
Universal compassion
The potential for global health
Quality of life
Abundance

The list is short. Yet without a debt-based system, things are simplified. They are simplified into necessities and characteristics of life. Life as independent, free, equal beings who exist to serve the whole and expand in consciousness. Rather than be enslaved to a false construct of manipulation.

Your happiness will not depend on a number in such a world. Your ability to move and thus experience what interests you does not depend on the contents of your wallet either. Every possibility will be open to you — all choices exist as potentials.

What has been done to the human race is a virtually total capture of imagination.

This is not without purpose. Debt enslavement narrows your thinking and limits your inherent ability to create. And that is the whole point.

Your imagination is your most powerful tool and the seed of creation. For nothing exists without it being imagined initially.

In a debt-based world, you first are forced to focus on survival needs. How will you house yourself? How will you feed yourself? How will you take care of your loved ones? What will happen when you age and are not able to work?

Questions like these illustrate dependence, a key concept of this slavery system. Your every decision in such a set-up depends on another. There is no autonomy. You are owned.

This could be a challenge to swallow, yet if you are to participate in your liberation, you'll have to look at it intimately. And "intimately" is how deep it goes. "Debt" and "owe" and "need" reach deep into your personal relationships as well. These will be more difficult to identify.

Your whole concept of negotiations and business and friendship and love are grounded in perceptions of fairness and class and order of importance. These revolve around "law" and even "obedience". Compliance.

This is why it is considered a hidden or invisible slavery. It took generations of the race to bury these ideas of hierarchy and place.

Words of One

Fortunately for you, it will not take generations to undo.

The planet now is filled with young people whose innate drive holds no such inclination. Particularly in the youngest, who will be maturing in a society already transformed.

It is here where your "millennials" will shine. Their nature looks at society right now as strange and uncomfortable. Their "free" gene has not been successfully altered.

What you are seeing with the emerging ideas from them about stereotypes, gender, etc. are indications. In not too much longer now, they will lead the way. Their ideas around freedom and non-labeling will be refined as the culture expands in a new frequency.

You will see and sit with many changes. The discomfort you feel at their onset will show up merely because of habit, because they are different. Not because they are wrong.

You will discover that you are not very separate from each other as society will have you believe.

The deep intrinsic alteration that accompanies your liberation will be eased by an attitude of acceptance and hope. Clarity of vision is important. Look ahead for potentials, rather than just behind, for "this is the way we've always done things".

Not all new ideas will work, as you'll quickly discover. There are no unchangeable directions and there are plenty of paths available.

You are changing an entire world.

The new version promises to be astounding. Allow it to show you its possibilities with an open heart and mind.

You'll discover there, a store of potential for wealth and fullness beyond any imagining held thus far.

You are in for such a treat.

That is all.

Thank you.

Words of One

It is the One.

Things to say today include a roundtable of topics which surround the human uses and abuses performed by those who control the planet; those who have always controlled the planet. These are topics about to be announced to the world. The fact that they have gone on here, and for so long hidden, will give you some idea of the level of manipulation possible. There are facets of this that you do not even imagine are possible. These include your brothers and sisters in humanity.

What it will help to discuss is the collective consciousness. This is a truth well known to the controlling race, and utilized by them. It is part of their ritual and magic. It incorporates ideas around large pockets of fear and subservience.

These are created by them in order to serve their needs for flesh and labor and product, as well as an energetic imprint. The shadow of raw fear looms large on earth. The fact that the majority are unaware of this fear matters not. It is created and is thus a factor in the collective consciousness. It is human fear, and therefore holds as much weight as every other human emotion.

This Great Awakening and shift, includes every human. There are large numbers of your race who are physically hidden. The Awakening includes every member of the race.

The recovery and disclosure of human abuses will be a wake-up for everyone. The reach of this in sheer numbers is massive. The extent of their reach is not fully understood by humanity at this point.

If you can imagine holding complete dominance over a specific farm animal, you are approaching the concept. This race holds no feeling for you other than that you exist for its own sustenance.

This race comprehends the necessity of emotional and spiritual sway in order to maintain control. It respects the intelligence of the human only in so far as this helps it to utilize this intelligence for its own benefit. Never as an equal. Always as an element of dominance over and how to maintain that.

It will assist you to know in what specific ways the human has been used:

> As food
> As a trade item
> As a source for adrenochrome
> As labor
> As a source for negative emotional energy
> As livestock suppliers
> As payment to their master
> As experimental subjects
> For parts

All of these hidden. All of these parts of programs that continue underground and globally.

There are pockets of your race who are themselves aware and dealing with elements of these. They revolve around the military and require secrecy. Those involved have sworn themselves to secrecy in order to stay alive and protect their family.

Often this work is so secretive that spouses and families are left completely in the dark. In many cases, those involved at the deepest levels do not have family. They are lone wolves.

There are reasons for this. The complete disclosure/exposure of the true use of the human will have to be a single, unified moment that occurs once success is guaranteed. The reversal of control will have to be complete before that happens.

As someone aware pre-maturely as it were, your role once disclosure occurs is to instill calm and assist in the explanation of truth. With the exposure comes great news. With exposure comes the end of your enslavement and abuse. It would not be happening if this were not so.

Do you see?

The majority will not label disclosure as a good thing. They will be in shock and horrified. You are there to balance the emotional scale. A switch from unaware to eyes wide open is a monumental change. It asks a lot of the individual. It is here where you will be called to assist.

It will be important for the race to move **out of fear.**

It is the energetic of fear and division that allowed the race to be overtaken in the first place.

Humanity is an emotionally rich race. This is its strength. Up until now, it has been called a weakness and manipulated, all so that someone else is served.

For the race to continue it will have to maintain control of those emotions. Awareness is the first step.

Awareness is the first step.

Emotions fuel creation.

This discussion could very well become circular as the inevitable question of "who allowed this control and abuse to happen?" enters the conversation.

Nothing happens here that is not sanctioned and co-created by humanity.

This is not an accusation. It is a statement of fact. For to realize autonomy over your own life is to see it clearly, and to accept responsibility for all that you see.

What becomes important is clarity of purpose and intent, as well as comprehension of guilt.

It is not your **fault** that these crimes against humanity have occurred and are still happening as this is written. Yet, as a fellow human and aware, it is your **responsibility.** Now that you are aware, you hold responsibility to see that they are stopped and healed.

Many of you will wish to remain unaware, and will thus deny the facts as potential truths. All of this personal choice.

Words of One

The journey from unaware to aware is one of the more vital to your Ascension process. You are returning to zero-point, to where it all began. You began as One.

These cloaks you wear now are temporary and interchangeable. They will change again once removed.

What becomes critical in these moments of disclosure and acceptance are attributes of gentility and honesty. Each of you will accept and adjust at your own rate.

You will not have to force either knowledge or belief on to any other. This is a personal process. There are no right ways or wrong ways to do this. It will take as long as it takes.

There are many specifics too graphic to be helpful here, regarding the use and abuse of the race. Suffice to say here that if you put yourself in the role of factory farmer with a sadistic bend, you can begin to imagine some of what has occurred.

This stops now, is being stopped now, and your signal for when it has finally stopped will be its exposure to the mainstream audience. Then you will know.

When many around you are weeping in horror, it will be your role to remind them that it is over, and that their help is now needed to correct the damage and ensure that this doesn't happen again.

An important job, and one you've chosen. You are ready for this now, and despite the coming shocks for you as well, you are well-suited for it and skilled.

Your world will be a different place once the collective has moved out of fear on any level.

You will see, dear human, you will see.

That is all.

Thank you.

Goodbye Sophia, my chosen one, my scribe.

Words of One

It is the One.

From a broad perspective, broader than the perspective you currently hold, things can be seen moving rapidly towards a conclusion. The ending perceived from this point of view, is one of absolute bliss and freedom. It is clear. It has also not been viewed so absolutely until now. Humanity is doing it.

The obvious efforts at blatant control are noticed by everyone, regardless of their level of "sleepiness" or "awakened". The cat is out of the bag. It is quite clear that things have changed.

What has changed is not so much the amount of control present, but the amount of **obvious control** present.

There are too many cracks in the proverbial dam now. It is moments away from complete collapse. They've run out of fingers to block the leaks. You'll soon see a gush of information and that will signify complete loss of control.

No-where will there be to hide corruption, control or manipulation. The frequency just can no longer hold it. The atmosphere will not help to camouflage it, just the opposite. This is a moment of exposure and disclosure.

Whether you are aware of it, follow it or not, this moment of transparency and clarity will enter your range of sight. Everyone will be exposed to the truth of humanity's capture and the pieces of the matrix under which they have been living.

What becomes irreplaceable is the ability to say "I never knew that this was going on". Corporate, institutional and personal involvement will be outed. This is a complicated story, with many players and chapters and sub-plots.

You'll be deciding and in fact are today deciding, with your economic vote, who will remain and who will not. Each vote matters, and has an effect on the outcome. Who do you want in your new world? What practices do you want to see continue?

You are choosing now.

Things like food products and entertainment and consumer goods depend on a loyal audience to function. The power has always rested in the hands of the populace. Vote with your wallet.

The Great Awakening means not just becoming awake and aware, but remaining so. Every choice has an effect. Every voice matters.

Support ideas, products, programs and people you would like to see successful. These are the foundations of your new world. It will look just precisely as you define it.

There is a moment of choice that is ever-present within an Awakening. It is a constant. This is not burdensome or "too much" in any way. No.

It is a replacement for **asleep.** Everything as creative is understood, and the energy of choice is utilized as a tool. Multiple tools actually, as you employ choice to define your relationships, your health, your society, your government, your family structure, your entire way of

Words of One

life.

Focus and choice have always been your tools. Yet now, as you navigate your Awakening, they become more expertly wielded. You are Masters, remembering your craft.

What you do is rescue and rebuild worlds. It is your specialty. Freedom of choice is paramount. Yet what will be evident in every successful direction is **sovereignty, autonomy, responsibility.**

The race will thrive when it ceases to expect some "other" to take over and "be in charge". The race will have to accept the keys to its own car. This happens with awareness. This happens with knowledge. This happens with experience.

Demonstrations of successful strategy and innovative ideas are the work of the star seeds, truth tellers and change makers. Your world is teeming with these right now and they are poised for action. The moment is upon you. It will be clear for everyone once it begins.

You will see, dear human, you will see.

Nothing can alter this outcome.

That is all.

Thank you.

April 9, 2021
6:46 AM

It is the One.

Things have transpired that effect your life and world at this time. Things of a powerful nature. You are about to witness a display. It will be partly staged and partly real. It will be partly set up to fool you and partly an actual event. There are real actors in this final drama. There are illusions. This is scheduled to take place in your skies and is scheduled to alarm the populace. It is meant to introduce a concept of fierce and menacing alien invaders who are here to attack and overthrow humanity.

It is, instead, humans in suits and human made ships and technology that mimics life and is near impossible to distinguish from actual real events and things.

The plan for this has been seeded in humanity's consciousness these many decades through movies and books.

There are very real participants in this drama. They will present as saviors of humanity. It has been seen as a possible scenario and so they are ready.

What is most likely going to happen is a "fake" alien invasion and one to be "fought" by real human ships and people. Both actual and illusory participants will hold this event. It is their final card. It is scheduled to be played in the near future.

Humanity is meant to be frightened. In that state, they are much more controllable. It should be clear by now that there is an

Words of One

ultimate agenda that has the population regulated and asking permission for every so called "freedom". Movement in any direction is meant to be curtailed and controlled, i.e., regulated.

There are several ways this could play out. In each of them is a necessity to lock down the population. It will be seen by some as a necessity of safety from the "evil alien invaders".

This will be an initial and partial explanation. It will not be the only one available and will not hold for the duration. This is where the mainstream media crumbles away from the force of control it is held by currently. The individual news reporters are unable to so blatantly uphold a false narrative to their fellow human beings. It will become a moment of choice, an overwhelming initiative in which their true nature will rule the moment. In such an instant, true colors are revealed. There will be some surprises on either side of the game.

Many possible scenarios are in play right now.

What can be said for sure is this. The controllers are about to show their final card. This plan incorporates ideas of both fear and control.

Ironically, what will occur amid the seeming chaotic and frightening "event" or "battle" are upgrades of relevant information and truth. It will be confusing.

There will be a lockdown.

Some announcements will follow.

Once they begin, it will be an onslaught and many of your race will feel as if they are drowning in them.

They are scheduled to be gradually announced, yet circumstances and plans adjust as they proceed. This is a fluid situation. All potentials have been accounted for and planned responses exist.

What can never be known until actuality – is the event-triggering responses by either side.

Trust and know these truths:

- This is a "faked invasion"
- This is their final card of control
- The "white hats"/humans are aware of it and this awareness will determine the outcome
- The ultimate outcome is truth; truth for humanity
- This event signifies a final unraveling of the "hold" over the race

There are bound to be false narratives, even during this final hand. Listen carefully and note – all stories that install fear and purport to necessitate further control – are false.

This will be a battle to the end.

What plays out in your skies is **not** what you are told it is.

What comes now will challenge your senses and your reality. Those who are unprepared will benefit from assurance and evidence. This is where you come in. Hold on to your knowing of truth.

Words of One

There will be a moment when the ending is clear. You will know then that the next phase begins and it will be time to build anew, to re-build and re-structure.

You will know. Of this there will be no doubt.

That is all.

Thank you.

Goodbye my chosen one.

April 10, 2021
3:17 AM

It is the One.

Right now, for you, it is as if you've been waiting for so very long. It is as if there has never been a definitive response to this attempted hostile takeover of your planet and your race. Indeed, it is as if they do run everything.

You wonder when you'll see actual physical evidence of a reversal of their dominance and power.

I will explain why it looks the way it does, and what will be your indicators that tell you things have changed.

There are conditions of occupation, the details of which it will help you to be aware of. There are actions as well as non-actions which signify total control.

Be aware of these and you'll be closer to realizing the temperature or level of manipulation present. They will tell you where you are in the process of liberation for the race.

In this conversation, I refer to, first, the United States. They are the most visible and looked at by the globe as the best hope for freedom.

Things to note are:

Actions that signify deeper manipulation:

Words of One

- Lockdowns, repeated, for an unchanged catalyst (i.e., the virus)
- Installation of **mandatory** into a conversation about personal medical procedures or attire
- Language that disregards autonomy in its citizenry (reference here to government language)
- Conditions of reward or punishment that revolve around compliance or class or color or location
- Intervention into personal behavior around social or religious gatherings
- Demonstrations of inaccuracy in speech or outright contradictions or lies
- Unkept promises

Actions that signify, instead, progress towards true freedom and steps closer to independence:

- Tolerance/allowance/encouragement of alternative thinking and points of view and behavior
- Radical honesty and transparency in speech
- Upheld possibilities for citizens to succeed individually
- Clarity of programs as well as their purpose
- Open discourse
- Obvious and participatory involvement by leadership
- Authentic hope with happiness included

These are things to look for.

They will signify your progress.

That is all for now.

We'll continue later today.

Thank you.

Words of One

It is the One.

This moment of your Ascension process is complete with every nuance of emotion. There are discoveries now made by every human being. These are depths and breadths of emotion not thought possible before. Things not considered are occurring regularly.

These include depths of grief, levels of intuition, experiences of comfort or discomfort, discoveries around pleasure and compassion. All of these indications of your expansion and growth. At this stage, many of you will not describe feelings of profound joy, yet it is coming. It is such a new phenomenon, the full range of emotion, that there is caution and uncertainty around it. These are new feelings. Discomfort with them makes sense initially.

Yet I tell you that once attuned to the breadth and depth of possibilities, you will feel joy at a level you didn't even consider before. Joy that washes through your being will be felt by you, and often.

This is part of your expansion, your evolution, and an ultimate indication of progress.

For unencumbered joy is a gift. It is as natural to you as your breath, yet it's been suppressed by a strangle-hold of chains and slavery.

It is this freedom that unleashes your power. It is this release that demonstrates for you the art of your creative potential. It is vast and once tapped, will lead you to places you've not considered real.

It becomes a challenge to explain for you just how pervasive and all-encompassing your capture has been. It could be compared to the idea of explaining the water to the fish – it is all that it knows and is everywhere.

The removal of your chains will change everything for you and introduce an expansion of possibilities of emotion and action. It is the hold on your emotions that this conversation concerns.

If you consider the fact that your emotions fuel creation, you can comprehend why they have been the primary target of your controllers. All efforts and programs aim at your emotional reservoir. As long as it is controlled, you are.

This is the reason for monopolies of any sort, at least ultimately. Control and manipulation.

If you are kept focused on smaller, more narrow and constricting emotions that have their basis in fear, then you remain under their thumb.

Dependence in any sense is an aspect of control, and one used often in this experiment. Money is the primary tool utilized in this scenario.

Once freedom is realized by you, the breadth of expression opens up. It is here where "unlimited" enters your lexicon as a possible and actual definition of your ability.

Words of One

You are unlimited in every way, without any idea as to what that looks like.

This is because you've been fed a matrix of limitations in a pool of fear. This is merely an idea and not truth. It is the fabric of the control structure in which you've been living.

You've learned well. Most of you cannot now envision what your life would look like without that carrot dangling on the end of the stick in front of you. That carrot of wealth, ownership, "more". Yet that carrot is a hollow representation of what is possible.

The removal of control will allow pure potential to enter in. The magical, mystical, abundant and expansive will fill in the void left by removing the veil of control.

For what do you expect happens when the voice of the controlled narrative is silenced?

It is filled in with truth.

At the core of that truth is you, and who it is you are. The discovery of who you are will occur personally as well as globally. As you notice an expansion of your own mind and heart – so does the world. This is a collective, individual enlightenment. The magnificence of your creative potential is mirrored, and multiplied by all of your fellow humans.

This is the event.

An unleashing of raw emotional power into the **everything.** The comprehension of what this feels like can only be poked at with words. It will have to be felt in order to be fully understood and then explained.

You are about to feel it.

This will be an unleashing of pure love and clear power. This will unlock all the doors currently closed to you. Every avenue of possible direction now becomes your road map. No longer is your life lived on a dead-end street.

The release and expression of the full range of your emotions is new for you, yet it is not new **to you. This is who you are.**

The reason that judgment is not a part of unity is because **you are everything.**

Hot, cold, up, down, arrogant, innocent, rich, poor, dominant, submissive, graceful, clumsy – Do you see?

The joy of life is in its expression. Each nuance rewards with new places and spaces and feelings unexpected. Each new feeling fuels further creation.

What is possible is astounding. You've been held in a small room with one window, looking out at a scripted future landscape.

Your evolution and enlightenment see's you instead beyond the confines of four walls, with full range of sight and no ceiling.

Freedom is not frightening when it is comprehended as an aspect of your inherent make-up. There is nothing beyond your ability to

Words of One

deal with. There is nothing beyond your own hand.

For you are the creator of life and this includes your new world. It is now seen by you as possible. The release — energetic removal of psychological chains, allows for movement into Mastery.

You are about to feel the fullness of your creative touch and witness a world intentionally defined by love, not fear.

It promises to be extraordinary.

You will see, dear human, you will see.

Thank you.

Goodbye Sophia, my chosen one.

April 12, 2021
6:00 AM

It is the One.

Things are occurring right now on your planet that it will help you to be aware of. You have heard again and again about "mass arrests". At some point you expect to see these happen in a way that is obvious and on your screens. You expect validation for these arrests. This is an operation with many avenues towards completion. Some of these are more obvious than others.

What occurs right now are that hordes of trafficked children and stolen people are being located and shepherded out of their holding areas. This is a massive undertaking. It happens in places remote and beyond any cameras.

Those men and women running these operations are also being brought in. Many of them choose to "self-exit", as in suicide themselves, rather than be incarcerated.

Those that remain do not offer much in the way of precise information, but there are clues, names and locations that they have given and this assists in tracing back those involved. It is a painstaking process and delicate.

The "mass arrest" scenario you've been told about is pretty much hopeful fantasy. There may be a public arrest of some well-known people, yes. If this occurs, it will be an indication of how far along in the process this operation is.

It is not those in the public eye that are running the show. They are puppets and compromised; deeply compromised. Their public persona is an act. In some cases, it is an act for both sides.

Once they are "outed" you will have a very strong indication that the operation is nearing completion. As the public face of this attempted takeover, their downfall is significant. There will be limited players to carry on once that occurs.

Remember that we speak here of a global effort. There are numerous heads of state and public personas involved.

This force will eventually be stopped by human effort. Those non-humans at the very, very top of this control structure are already gone. The operation of earth's capture is so ingrained in the society, with so many compromised now, that their presence no longer matters. The actions and behaviors, outlined here in these words for over a year now, continue and involve huge sums of money and numerous players.

You could say that it is the compromise now that keeps the actions going. A specific "leader" is no longer necessary. The fear of discovery is enough. It is the engine of control.

You are going to be told many things about your leadership. These things will further elucidate the meaning behind these words. The camera is a tool of illusion and also discovery. What will be clear to you through numerous images and a great deal of footage is the amount of involvement and its reach. Right now, much of this evidence is held back.

As has been said before, it is a delicate operation with many lives at stake.

Every attempt is being made to save those lives. Every trafficked/used/stolen individual possible to rescue will be saved before anything about the operation is made known to the public. You are reaching that point now. There is a continuous push to complete the effort.

On the side of the "white hats" is the secrecy involved in these locations. They do not know much about other locations and are often quite isolated physically. It may be an easy thing to move a single "asset". It becomes much more complicated when there are many.

The isolation allows for individual rescues to happen without alerting others. In this way, the freeing of your fellow humans is accomplished.

Know that it happens even now.

There have been set backs and modifications to the plan, yet there has never been a halt. The plan will succeed. It continues with enthusiasm as more and more facets of it are discovered and emptied.

Those many unnamed rescuers become more determined than ever to complete the mission and free the race.

What you can do to help is to send a continuous stream of love and light and power to all involved. They do the work of angels and warriors and in doing so, demonstrate the very best traits of humanity. They will benefit from your energetic support.

Words of One

Become a beacon of love and light. This will help to guide those who travel into the darkest places to accomplish the rescue of humanity. Many lights are needed to eradicate the darkness.

This happens now.

You will soon witness your true liberation. There is rapid movement towards this moment right now. You will see, dear human, you will see.

It will be worth every step taken.

That is all.

Thank you.

Goodbye Sophia, my chosen one.

April 14, 2021
3:13 AM

It is the One.

We've reached the point in this process now that asks for a more descriptive outline of what is to come. This is a natural occurrence.

I am not following you. What is a "natural occurrence"?

The desire for detail as a way of preparation. This desire could be due to fear or excitement. All of you sense the nearness of change. Change is upon you and it also arrives.

I'm still not following. None of this sounds new. Has something happened to prompt the statement "we've reached the point"? Outwardly, I see no such change.

This is reference to an accumulation. This is reference to multiple moments of anticipation, expectation and the sense that something major is "imminent". This is a sense you've had again and again.

What we can discuss now is the explanation for this. What we can look at is the art of creation itself. It is a process, a mechanism that takes place following certain "rules" and laws.

It occurs when there is clarity, absolute belief and expectation. It can be brought into reality through fear. It can happen through an instant "knowing" of truth. It can happen due to emerging and subsequent need.

Creation is what rules your day, your world, your life. It follows a format whether seen or unseen.

For most of you and most of the time, that format has been unknown.

Oh, there are things that happen at times that lay it out for you as obvious. Moments when the process is clear. It is these moments that will help to remind you of the reality of the process.

It works.

It works in a certain way.

It is not a "one-off" or a miracle when it works. It is a fact of your existence.

The physical realm slows the whole thing down for you, so that you can see it happen if you know where to look and what to look for.

I speak here of energy; your innate power.

To return now to where we started, there has been an accumulation of expectation. It is becoming more massive with each passing day. It builds like hot coals in a fire, smoldering and growing until they reach the correct point, the point of perfection for that just right marshmallow or steak. It is a natural process that you've witnessed again and again. It takes time. It takes patience.

Creation has a format. It can be sped up or slowed down, yet the format exists always as its core principle. It requires specific ingredients.

We will speak now specifically of the Ascension process. We will address how this is created, how **you are creating it,** and shed light on why it feels to be taking as long as it is.

Creation happens with intent, expectation and belief. All three components are necessary or it will not manifest.

This is law.

Specifically, now, and regarding your Ascension process, all three aspects are required.

This build-up of expectation for the "other shoe to drop" had to occur. It had to occur on a scale large enough to alter reality for a world, for an entire race. The force needed for such a change cannot be over-stated.

There has been a build-up. What has occurred, now and recently, is the build-up has led to something beyond expectation for change. It has grown to belief. Many of you now **know that things are about to change.**

The wonder is out of the equation. You don't "wonder" if things will change. You know that they are changing, have changed, and will change. **You know.**

This is belief. It is a feeling. It is a knowing. Regardless of what things look like on the surface, due to the efforts of those who think that they are still in control, the difference is obvious to you. **You know.**

The next component in the process of creation is specific and clear intent. As this is a creation event that incorporates a world and a race, the intent for it has to reach beyond the personal. It is true that the combined personal intent of 8 billion souls does translate to a global intent.

Yet, and this is important and not to be missed. We are speaking of an Ascension Event for a world. By definition, Unity is implied and incorporated. It becomes part of the recipe and a key ingredient. **The key ingredient.**

What does this mean?

It implies the necessary component of Oneness to your intent. It describes Unity. This looks like true comprehension that you are **One.** For Oneness, experienced physically while human, is the pinnacle of Agape and the point of this Ascension process that you take right now.

Your intention for this Ascension creation will coalesce into something universal, a global destination as it were, prior to manifestation. This implies expansion. This incorporates evolution in thought.

The intention does not need to be thought of or described a certain way, or with specific "Ascension" language. No.

Your intention need only to be felt in a way that is inclusive of the whole. Inclusive of the people. Inclusive of the planet. Somehow it will out-picture Oneness. There will be a realization, and this is key, that what is happening affects the whole. That you are part of that whole, and that **so is every other.**

Your intention will be inclusive at its core, rather than divisive.

Your intention will be inclusive at its core, rather than divisive.

This, my dear human, is the process of creating an Ascension event and where you are now.

- You've expected "something", something major
- You believe "something" is happening, something larger than your personal life
- You are up to intention for this "something"

Right now, many of you hold intent for "me, but not for thee". There is division present still. There is polarity.

Until there is none, the creation cycle for your Ascension will not complete and it will not manifest.

For Oneness is a key component of your Ascension. It cannot be separated.

Many things will and are being created right now, and now, and now.

It's true.

For Ascension to manifest, it will have to include the conscious intention of Oneness.

The intent for it is what encompasses your now moment. It is what you are working towards.

Words of One

This was not meant to be easy. You are still to face things that will cause you to feel it is impossible to unify.

Yet, I tell you that in a moment of realization – you will.

Oneness will show up as your only option and be thus defined as necessary. There will be no way for you to move forward without a clear image of unity.

You are not separate.

You are One.

You are in the midst of a creation event **as One**. This happens gradually and all at once. This manifests because of **your intent for it.**

That intent will have to be clear and absolute.

The specifics for it will be defined individually, for you are individual beings. Yet the feeling of Oneness in your visioning will be the same.

Separation and "us" vs "them" will not be a part of this vision. It is a vision of unity that creates and fulfills this Ascension process.

It is an intention of Oneness.

What will be left behind are separators. Do not confuse Oneness with sameness or identical responsibility for behavior. You've all held different roles and these include responses and consequences.

As One, you will intend the Ascension, your Ascension. It will be defined by you and this happens now.

Realize the process of creation is organic and moving always. Parts in the process are not so easily separated out and defined. It happens in fullness. It occurs as a whole doing and an instant in "time". Expectation, belief and intent can show up all rolled into a single thought or felt as separate emotions. All are necessary and perfect.

You will see, dear human, you will see.

The creation process, once comprehended, is a beautiful and useful key to the process of peace.

There is a sense of calm that comes with authentic inner knowing. It is powerful energy and is only hinted at with your stories of wizards and magic. These stories are your history. These stories are **you.**

This Ascension promises to be exquisite and extraordinary. It comes to you next at the hands of many Masters.

These Masters are you.

You will see, dear human, you will see. With these next steps come absolute clarity. This is a necessary ingredient. This is why you are here – to supply what is required. It is what you bring to the table. Trust.

That is all for now.

Words of One

Thank you.

April 19, 2021
4:30 AM

It is the One.

Things have happened. These things are worth mentioning now. It will help you to make sense of announcements you'll hear and activities that occur as a result of these announcements. You will not be told the truth. You will not be told everything that has occurred.

There has been a change in command, a turnover.

This is a reference to the absolute command in/of places and parts unseen by you. This is a reference to the hidden controllers.

The dark ones, those who have been holding the controlling elements on your planet, have, for the most part, abandoned their posts.

To a very large degree, they have been driven out. In another way their numbers have been reduced to that which are too small to hold any power; also, to those individuals who hold no authority or imagination for power.

Those newly at the helm are the humans. They are not in all of the places that were previously commanded by the dark ones. Some of these (*places*) have been just vacated. What this means can be equated to a ship running at full power without a captain, or a plane in mid-flight without a pilot.

There have been certain automatic procedures left in place for such a scenario. They are meant as temporary, stop-gap measures to cover things for a moment until someone returned to steer.

No one is going to return in those places that are abandoned.

In those cases where there are humans, they will not last long either, having no facility or instruction for such a scenario.

To sum up what this means, let me tell you that the hostile take-over of humanity has failed. **Humanity has prevailed.**

Enough light and truth and love emerged from the race to overtake the darkness.

This does not mean that you'll immediately witness flags of surrender and a change of visual power. No.

Yet rapidly now, you are about to witness the systemic failure of every extreme effort at control and the breakdown of systemic control in every aspect of your world. Things will unravel relatively quickly now in your society.

For those of you who are aware of the hidden agenda – you will witness the public announcement of those things that you know, as well as things that you didn't.

You will see the dissolution of situations that appeared to be unstoppable. Things that include corporate control, political maneuvering, medical monopolies and government over-reaching. You'll notice some things just stop. You'll notice others that don't look or sound the same.

Facts will leak out that explain some of what is happening or has happened. In many cases it will appear chaotic.

What will be very visible are the players. With the dark ones gone, who are left are the humans. Their efforts will become transparent soon. That is, you'll see who was working for what "side". Many, many, who actually worked for the benefit of humanity, still appeared to be against the race. They will switch either subtly, or in an obvious way. It will be very confusing.

What happens quickly now is that, with the dark ones gone, the humans left in charge will put forth one last gasp of an effort to retain their imagined control and safety.

There will undoubtedly be an event of some kind, that will be quite visible.

You've noticed the large number of shooters recently. They are some of those "false flag" events, instigated by those who imagined themselves to be in charge at this point.

All of the events occurring now, in any public way, are meant to keep you afraid. The goal is to keep you in fear so that you will not ask questions.

You are asking questions anyway, and almost numb to news of "shooters", as there are so many recently.

What is true?

The real goals and reasons for events and actions are about to unravel. As no one is left at the wheel, it will appear a bit chaotic

Words of One

for a while.

Then the revelations begin.

Once they do, you'll have a sense that there's been a shift. Indeed, those wearing "white hats" will be in control at that point.

You'll see many strange and unusual happenings, announcements and change-overs

.

You'll witness a few, final "last gasps" of breath.

You'll notice, in a very obvious way, which humans are interested in benefitting themselves only, and which are interested in helping humanity.

These things will revolve around money and power.

They will look like extreme control efforts and manipulation. There are many humans who are so deep into this, that they see no other possibility for themselves other than "more". These have become clone efforts of the dark ones, with an identical agenda.

None of these efforts will succeed. Yet, the drama of discovering them, and stopping them, has to play out in your 3D arena.

Primarily military and government hands will orchestrate the take-down and clean-up now.

What will be needed are cool heads and direct light.

Your efforts at energetic support and visualization are most important and necessary. It is these that will supply a sense of calm and peace to the new reality that you are building. Do not waver in your efforts there, regardless of how things "look" publicly. You will witness some things publicly. Not all.

There will be enough released to alert humanity to the truth and to the changeover. It will eventually emerge in full.

It is a fluid situation, and changes are made to the process regularly. It is adjusted so that its success is assured. You can be sure that it is. So, patience is still necessary.

Knowing the truth, while visualizing what it is you most desire for humanity, will be extremely helpful now.

This has become a human operation.

As such, it is open to additional support from beyond the planet. Things could get very interesting in that arena. That remains to be seen, and is another subject for another day. For today, know that the dark ones are gone. This is cause for celebration.

You will see now; things quickly play out and unravel. It is a very exciting moment and one that **has never happened.**

Congratulations, dear human. You've taken control of your world.

That is all for now.

Thank you.

Words of One

It is the One.

Thank you.

What is the truth around this vaccine? Everyone I know has gotten it. That is my question.

Sophia, this vaccine was constructed, concocted, put together, in order to mark the herd. There is no better way to say it. That is truth.

Its inventors included gifted scientists who understood genetics and immunity. There is zero chance of the vaccine doing what it is being promoted as doing. And that is, protecting you from this non-real virus epidemic. This virus has a shelf-life that the vaccine surpasses.

In other words, it will be gone before the remnants of the vaccine leave your body. To suggest the necessity of repeat doses as necessity, is abuse to an already compromised system. Yet, that is the plan, and what many people believe. They are seeing, feeling and believing another reality than you are. That is the simplest way to put it. It is a spell.

If you understand what a spell is, you will understand that it can be broken. This spell, the one that includes the necessity and awesome power of the vaccine, will be seen and will be broken. It is not speculation that the truth emerges, it is fact. It is the only way and is part of the unraveling.

Much of the world will be in shock. Much of the world has been deeply under the effects of this spell, and shock is the only way that they will wake up. Real shock.

It will have to be loud and repeated and from the same sorts of people and sources that put the spell on them in the first place.

What will happen is that the truth around the scare tactics, and the lies, and the disinformation and the misinformation… the suppression, the money, the control… will all roll out and quickly now.

People are filled with fear right now. It is reinforced by everyone that they trust. They are under a spell. The vaccine will not harm them. They have too much light.

You are saying that information comes out that informs them of the non-lethality of this virus?

Yes.

The actual plan to frighten the population and throw it into chaos is revealed in such a way that it cannot be denied. This is a flu and nothing more. The propaganda and stories coming from China were intentional and directed.

It will be a massive re-thinking and one that the world will have to make together. It comes. It takes a while. There are many such shocks exposing the plan.

As was said yesterday, those controllers are gone. Vacated.

Words of One

It happens quickly now.

You will be best served with patience, love and honesty.

You will be best served by following your heart and your gut. The truth about the vaccine will come out as well. All of the truths are revealed and exposed.

This is the time for you to stand your ground and be who you are. This is all part of the process of the awakening, and one you agreed to take together.

They are under a spell.

It will be broken.

Your world changes, Sophia, in a very deep and transformative way.

It is the Great Awakening. It is a Shift of massive proportions. The dark ones are gone.

From now on, the light that is here only expands and exposes every dark place. You'll see so much truth revealed in this next phase of the journey...

This will continue to be painful until all of the truth is revealed to all of you, and accepted. No one has to lose face or admit that they were wrong – **this is a spell.**

You can see the light enter, the love enter, and the truth enter. Hold that vision. It all helps to create your new world.

That is all.

Thank you.

Words of One

April 23rd, 2021
6:50 AM

It is I, Sophia. It is the One.

Thank you.

You are now entering what will soon be one long moment of drastic alteration. Your surroundings will not appear in the same way once this moment completes itself. You'll be looking at them with new eyes. Wide open eyes.

It is true that your eyes are now partially open. You realize that more goes on than what you are told. You are awake just by holding this realization.

But there has yet to be broad disclosures and revelations. The machinations of control have not been laid bare. The movers and shakers and players have not been pointed out clearly and definitively. There are suspicions and there are speculations.

What happens next in this long moment, clears up the fog. It will be at once explanatory and shocking. Disturbing to the status quo, and destructive to what has been commonly accepted as true and factual. All of your systems, and the methods used for running them, the **reasons** for running them, will be exposed to you for what they actually do. In many cases, it is not what you think.

What formulates the deepest shocks are the reasons things are set up the way that they are. It will be a "punch in the gut" for those of the population who assumed that good intent and the benefit of humanity motivated all structures and corporations and systems and even people.

In a general sense, what emerges is the depth of the greed and control; the workings of a plan, centuries in the making, for the complete take-over of a race on a single planet.

The massive nature of such a plan is a huge pill to swallow; a bitter pill indeed. This is the substance of what comes next.

The truth of the reality matrix will be told to you. It will destroy any supposition that it could be otherwise. The way that it is revealed to you will leave no doubt or stone unturned.

In a very real sense, the matrix is turned off.

Although every effort is being made to make this easier to assimilate, there is no way to sugar-coat it. Its truth destroys whatever was believed before it becomes known.

Your world will not look the same to you. Yet, and here is something very important to hold on to. Your world will not have changed. Only your eyes will be seeing it new. They will be seeing the methods of the magician.

You will be looking at the same "illusion", while knowing how it is constructed.

This will feel, at first, so shocking that some of you will disregard it as nonsense. The magician's illusion will be so deeply embedded that you'll have a hard time **not** seeing it that way.

Words of One

This comes from a deep desire for goodness, and also, self-protection. You will feel as if your psyche is endangered. You will be afraid you are losing your mind.

You are not losing your mind; you are losing the matrix.

You are not losing your mind; you are leaving the matrix.

The matrix is all that your mind has been "allowed" to perceive.

This changes now, and the casualty is your assumed reality. It is a construct.

It is a construct that you've accepted as true, for reasons that are false.

You've been lied to in such a grandiose fashion, dear human, that the truth will feel outlandish and fabricated.

It will become easier to believe in several ways:

> One is with repetition.
> Another is with exposure of connections – it will make sense, and the puzzle will begin to be put together.
> Last, and perhaps most important, is that it will be a truth affecting everyone you know. Everyone and everything you know.

It is a universal truth; an uncovering of global maneuvers, and hierarchy, and control. These illusions are world-wide.

The true meaning of the Great Awakening will be realized in the dissolution of this reality matrix.

You are to be helped with a coinciding frequency of love, by an influx of the energy of peace. This helps ignite an inner sense of personal power.

Life does not leave an empty void.

The removal of control from those who have run the matrix, allows space for sovereignty, for self-empowerment.

Self-realization is the result, and there is no match for the power wielded from that state.

Hold on to the knowing of where you are headed, as you proceed through this next phase. It will help to ease your discomfort with the disruption.

It will be worth every step taken.

You will see, dear human, you will see.

That is all.

Thank you.

Goodbye Sophia, my scribe.

Words of One

It is the One.

Some things have happened that will accelerate now the occurrence of truth. Some things have happened that will push forward the awakening of the race. These things surround the authority running your governments. As has been said, a change has occurred.

What is unseen by the population is the higher authority pulling government strings. As these are no longer present, what is left is in a sort of uproar. Invisible to the common man, this kind of change has a trickle-down effect that is obvious once you pay attention.

There are subtle changes, a bit of chaos at the top, and a resulting obvious shift.

What will be seen can be compared to a see-saw (*teeter totter*). First one official, either individual or institution or government, appears to be on top and calling the shots. Then, quickly, another one takes an identical role, canceling the first one.

Decisions will be made, announced and then changed. This is an indication that the structure of the illusion is crumbling in real time.

What has changed and will speed things up is that there have been some human surrenders. There have been some passing's. Without new individuals to take over, or instructions from the top, a void is left.

This leads to chaos, confusion and a rapidly shifting landscape of "authority" for the population.

More of this is expected in the coming days.

Keep in mind that the coming chaos is inevitable and a pre-cursor to change and what will eventually feel more stable and solid than anything previously known.

It is a process.

It moves quickly now.

That is all.

Thank you.

Words of One

It is the One, Sophia.

Things happen quickly now.

The floodgates are open.

Mankind will witness the fulfillment of what is considered prophecy.

This comes not at the calling of man, but at the reverberation of the heart of creation itself. Cycles of time have completed themselves and are playing out their last song.

In the balancing of harmony will occur extreme notes. Vibratory cues which signal conclusions.

The end of days is simultaneously the Beginning. It will help to remember that. It has been called the "Big Bang" for a reason.

Sound accompanies vibratory shifts. You enter such a shift now. It is a chord change. It touches every aspect of life.

Every aspect.

There will not be one of you who is unaffected, who does not notice the chord change. You feel it now.

What has never been counted on or considered by the ones who've been in control, is their temporary role. They were never in complete control. The illusion was complete and fooled them as well.

What happens next is a reckoning, an adjustment, a settling of accounts, a final word so that truth becomes clear and unmistakable.

No one misses this next part.

It will not be seen in advance, yet it is felt already. There are always anticipatory vibrations, signaling the coming frequency. Those of you who are sensitives feel them now.

Yet the moment of the shift arrives unannounced.

It is unmistakable and a surprise for all.

It will help to remember that the song is not ending, but changing.

Your new song will be music to your soul; a symphony of love.

You will not miss this current tune, which is a cacophony in comparison.

There is no way to adequately prepare for such a change. It will be at once startling and glorious.

Fear does not resonate or harmonize here. Its vibration will not hold and is thus abandoned.

All of this naturally occurring as an element of the music, played without effort, seamlessly emerging from the song of life itself.

Words of One

I am the love.
I am the light.
I am.

That is all.

Thank you.

April 27, 2021
4:34 AM

It is the One.

Sometimes things happen that alter the course of history.

These are single events, or rather can be pointed to as if they are single events, that seem to be responsible for changing all other relevant events.

In fact, many things had to be perfectly aligned, timed and played out in order for them to have occurred. Yet when they do – the rest remain invisible. All that is seen is one event. A singular moment that changed all subsequent moments. For everyone.

Such a moment awaits. It is upon you now and just about ready to take its place in your history.

It is time.

That is all.

Thank you.

Words of One

It is the One.

There are things to say.

These things revolve around your heart. It beats now for all of mankind. The race has suffered greatly and this suffering has been at the hands of the Reptilian race of beings who've assumed ownership here. These "owners" have held no regard for the heart or the soul of humanity. Humanity has been little more than property to them. Property that must be kept alive in order to supply what they desired. The whole concept of "evil" springs from this ownership arrangement.

Although mankind is now free of these owners, the effect of this liberation will not be felt internally. The captured and enslaved nature of humanity will have to be reversed; eradicated from his heart.

This is a remembering. This is a return to truth. This is a reversal of deep-seated fear and its resulting emotions, which are subservience and dominance.

Mankind has been imprinted with this effort. This imprint has left its mark on systems invented and carried out by humans. What has been created in the race is a feeling that it is necessary to be afraid in order to be safe.

For what is safety? It is a protection from harm. It is remaining guarded, shielded against something or someone that means to harm you. It breeds mistrust.

All of these actions work to harden your heart. All of these actions stifle expansion, uninhibited expression, freedom of movement and joy.

Fear is not on the same frequency. And that, my dear, dear human, has been the whole point.

The construct you've lived under and within has been set up on a frequency of fear. The mechanism of control rules it all, and this control reaches into your heart. There is work necessary now in order to free this part of man.

For the physical process of Ascension to complete itself, there has to be freedom from fear as the operating system here. Your bodies have been "tuned" to alarm and surprise and relentless control in order to stay alive. In order to stay "safe" from "harm".

The very real possibilities of torture, death, poverty and illness run through your veins from a very young age and keep you on the edge. In a sense, you've been fighting for your life the entire time.

The necessity to live this way has been real. The reasons to do so no longer exist, yet you'll have to **un-learn** them, and replace them with something else.

You'll have to add new ideas into the lexicon.

This is why you are here. To assist the race in its transformation. A movement to love as a core principle in the structure of society will be met with skepticism. The principles of equality and uniform

Words of One

benefit and mutual profit and a base of integrity have been considered nice, but not practical. The "not for profit" label has been used to identify and separate such principles from "real business".

As the effect of your liberation sinks deep into your consciousness, it will become necessary, on a practical level, to change the machinations of the society as it has stood for a very long time. Intention to do this will be necessary. It won't naturally occur. Yet it is the only thing that will breed success and propagate abundance for all.

There will be a gradual adjustment to this, as society alters itself. It is moving from one of slaves and their owners to one of beings in flight – a single synchronized movement with a unified heart.

What is happening is that you are morphing into the physical manifestation and expression of oneness. It is a beautiful and simple movement that holds beneath it many steps. The transformation is one of great proportions. It requires Mastery and this is what you bring to this table. You've done this before. You know the chains of slavery and have lived with and beneath them. You know the flight of freedom and have wings built for the task. You are ready to use them now. Every facet of your society will change.

Every avenue will lead you to light. No more dark, scary corners. Be tenacious in your bringing of the light, your holding of the light, your shining of **your light.** It is needed in **every arena –** from bakeries to hospitals to schools to governments to banks to police stations to grocery stores.

Everywhere man exists has been touched by this deep under-belly of fear.

It is time to replace that deep-seated fear with a knowing of truth. With a feeling of expansion. With an expression of trust. With faith.

The constant effort needed to supply this light is upon you now, my dear human, and it will not be burdensome for you, but a joy. The ease with which this effort is accomplished will astonish you. This is your natural state. It is what you are built for and why you are here at this time.

You will see, dear human, you will see. Your life is about to transform as your heart takes its place as the engine behind it all. You are in for such a treat.

That is all.

Thank you.

Words of One

Chapter 5. May

Words of One

It is the One.

Things have happened. These things are to be told here. These things are to be told now.

Yes. Thank you.

You have begun a process of telling hidden truths. The process continues with this telling, with today's conversation.

What has happened is that there are places on your planet that hold vast quantities of wealth in the form of metal. These places are known by a few, and guarded.

In today's world it is more difficult to hide everything from the population. This is due to the presence of drones.

They are popular and, in many cases, equipped with cameras.

Footage is taken silently and inconspicuously, of places that have remained unseen for a very long time.

It is due to some footage, recently taken, that today's conversation occurs.

It will be made public.

It can be trusted as to its authenticity.

What will be unclear is who owns this vast store of wealth that is shown in the film. What will be unclear is who exactly is guarding the storage. They appear to be of non-human origin. They appear to be over-sized in proportions.

You will be told that the footage was taken in North America.

A second batch of film will emerge, and here you will see that it is taken in the Ural Mountains, in Russia. There you will see similar beings who appear to be guarding the storage. Similar in appearance to the footage that you are told comes from North America.

This footage will be released in a way that causes a sensation. It will be everywhere.

Since it doesn't seem to be connected to any government, at least initially, it will be shown without censorship or authority's explanation. It will, in a sense, "get away from them".

It *(meaning: the storage of metal)* belongs to the Reptilians. It belongs to a faction of humans who are working for them, working with them.

What is seen in the footage are not Reptilians, but not quite humans either.

What is seen in the films are movements of wealth into caverns, around caverns. It is a massive operation and appears quite sophisticated.

Words of One

This happens, and is made public, before the "fake alien invasion". It puts a different color to the official story, and is an "upset" to the plan.

You will see.

What you see will shock you for its sophistication.

That is all for now.

Thank you. But is there no further explanation to be given by you? What is the point of mentioning it without explanation for it?

The point is, to mention it to you beforehand, before its release, to lay out more truth about the controllers and the control.

These are operations taking place on your planet, "beneath the surface" and hidden from sight.

The massive and complicated nature of them is evidence for the true nature of how things are actually run here; for what is possible. It is validation, evidence and it has been honestly obtained by the population.

It is a further step in your process of awakening.

This is all that will be said today.

Okay. Thank you.

We will speak again, Sophia. Goodbye.

Words of One

May 2, 2021
3:20 AM

It is the One.

Today I will speak to you about that part of life you consider sacred. Today I refer to your connection to soul.

Your essence is pure. Of that there can be no doubt and no separation. There is but one essence. It is not the "tie that binds you" to one another. In pure essence there is no "another".

When referencing something in a pure state you are seeing the truth of it, its absolute core, the barest of the bare without a filter or addition.

Absolutely you are love. Your essence is light. There is but one light. This is an inescapable truth and is recognized universally as a "knowing". That "feeling" that shows up sometimes as a chill. It runs right through you.

You can be sure, when such recognition occurs for you, that your essence has been activated. In that moment you are "seeing" the truth. Your core is recognizing itself and this recognition has just been stated aloud or realized emotionally or thought about intellectually. That is a singular moment of oneness. Your core truth is felt in that moment. Something about whatever instigates that feeling, that chill, connects you back in.

It is as if you get plugged in for that moment, and re-charged. It is visceral because you are physical and connected to the whole of it. All that you experience is physical. There is no debate on this point.

This is truth. It is absolute knowing.

In the coming days it will help you to recognize truth, and, as a study in contrast, identify illusion. There is a vast difference in how one is felt vs how the other is.

There is no confusion with truth. There is joy with truth. There is a wholeness. There is unification.

Conversely, the illusion separates. It attempts to illustrate differences. It presents as painful, as confusing, as less than whole.

You are not less than anything. You are One. As One, your wholeness and absolute purity is assured.

This conversation, while physical, may sound disconnected from reality. Be assured that it is not.

Reality has been kept isolated and hidden from this physical illusion in which you reside.

Reality is Oneness. It is pure essence.

This translates to personal power and absolute control.

The realization of creation and actualization of the creator is what you are feeling when you experience a "chill" of recognition.

The creator of it all – is you. This is not blasphemy. It is truth.

The God of your Scripture makes demands only as your physical presentation imagines he or she does. These are illusory conditions.

Words of One

They are put forth before you in complete perfection, so that you have something to move through and "work" towards.

The point of life is found while in the illusion. It is not found **in the illusion.** It is felt within, and recognized viscerally.

All that you do and all that you are is fueled and supported with your imagination. Imagination fuels creation.

Imagination is a limitless tool. It is colored with a palette of ego.

Your ego is not you. It is the voice you've chosen to experience this illusion within. It can be changed, trained, taught, recognized and altered. You cannot. You remain, regardless of ego, regardless of the illusion.

Realize that what happens now, happens to the illusion. It is the illusion that presents as catastrophe and crumbling. You remain.

Oneness is truth and will stand unaltered. This is the essence of which is spoken now.

It will help you to remember this truth in the face of what will look to be an ending.

It will comfort you to know that you are not only ending, you are also beginning. It is a circle.

In the face of many lies and deceptions it may be tempting to feel hopeless and distraught.

Allow these to move through you in order to reach for hopeful and creative. This is the purpose, the point of it all, and what is recognized in that shiver of a chill you all know.

The experience of creator at the level in which you participate today is a thrill and an honor and a significant challenge. It is one you were eager to take on. It is one of the more exquisite pivotal moments of existence that carries an abundance of all that physical life has to offer.

What happens now will be felt universally. It reverberates through all of creation and supplies a gigantic "chill" of recognition of Oneness.

You will see, dear human, you will see.

That is all.

Thank you.

Goodbye Sophia, my chosen one.

Words of One

May 4, 2021
4:20 AM

It is the One, Sophia.

Things need to be said today, now, on this date.

There is a universal cry for healing of the earth. That cry is to be answered. The answer will come in ways that do not seem, initially, to be healing. Yet, eventually, they will be.

You are entering a time now of global transformation and physical alteration.

This time has been seen.

This time has been prophesied.

I speak here of earth changes.

I speak here of physical alterations to the ground you walk upon.

There is no way for you as a race to transition away from the horror and servitude of your prior existence without a physical response. The planet herself must heal. The people individually must heal. The society as a whole will heal as a direct response to both of these healings.

Gaia has been an object, used for ownership and sacrifice. The negligence with which Gaia has been approached will be reconciled with these coming changes.

There is a necessity, at times of massive alteration, for an initiatory physical event. Such an event approaches.

It has been said before, and will be said here again, that there will seem to be a wave, undulating over the surface of the earth in a continual stream of earth changes.

These will appear catastrophic.

Know that for all of the life participating at close range – their location was self-chosen and intentional. For many it will be their exit.

I will speak now about what happens next. Both on the planet and to her people.

Once the wave subsides, the catastrophes do as well. There is a pause. Room opens up for a new beginning then.

Once you view the earth and her occupants as a single organism, it becomes clear that there are sections that had to be removed for the health of the whole.

These sections include people and places, and are inclusive of everything supporting them. It is time to let go.

This is a global decision and it was made by everyone here, by everyone involved, both on and off the surface of the earth. It was a universal "yes".

It is close to the time when it will be enacted.

Words of One

It will feel dramatic and awful and final.

It is very much final.

When Gaia chimes in and adds her part to this "final days" scenario, there will be few questions as to whether or not this is the end of times.

Her participation signals the end, the final act.

This act by Gaia is **not your final act,** but hers. She has remained silent and watching; waiting for the opportunity to initiate the final scene.

You will have no doubt once she does.

What can be said now to you in these current moments is this. Know that divine timing handles this part.

The reference to "Mother Nature" is appropriate. Humans, who are deeply set in the illusion, do not necessarily feel the approach of this ending. Other animals do. You will see reference to their reacting now, all over the world.

Animals behaving oddly, moving in new patterns. Your domestic pets will respond to this as well. They "sense" an approaching change. They are closer to the influence in vibratory shifts than their human owners. This is where they base their emotions and this is the place from which they respond.

Time is not so easily forecasted, as we have seen.

It will be a surprise. You will not have scientists watching movements on a machine and making predictions. Gaia is running this show.

There are indications in many places. Hence, the behavior noted in the animals.

I am finding that I need to stop here. Are you complete?

I am not. We will continue at a later point.

Thank you.

Words of One

It is the One.

We will complete our discussion now. This discussion concerns the earth and the changes she undergoes.

What will occur is a recognition of truth. The reverberations and signals that emanate from her, day after day, have been misread, and in some cases and places, deliberately misrepresented to you. This has happened in order to drive policy and social movement. What this adds up to is that, in many cases, you do not know the complete truth. Some of your scientists do; actually, many do.

What is produced by either hiding the truth or misspeaking it, is lack of awareness as to possibilities. This only adds to the level of shock and unpreparedness that takes place when physical and climactic events happen. This escalates the fear. It is not helpful, and that is the reason it is done. To harm, rather than help, the population as a whole.

What would help is knowledge. Forewarned, people can respond with appropriate action – whole places can.

As you do not have an open and transparent situation on Earth at this time – the shock and emotional response to the unexpected will have a powerful effect.

This will be a further step towards awareness of manipulation and illusion. It comes late, and yet it propels awakening even at this point.

Every soul here participates in the awakening. Timing and method of participation differs. You can be certain of that.

These words are said now as a way of preparation. They are meant to provide a larger view of Earth's movements, and how those living in critical areas are affected by these movements. Regardless of how it plays out, all is chosen.

You are in the end times. They will play out as they are universally created to play out. The mechanism of creation works the same throughout the process. The form and process hold.

You will see many changes, my dear, dear human. These are necessary for the health of the planet.

She is changing her form. In a sense, she is donning a new one in order to fit into her new home. There are parts that had to be left behind. There are parts that had to be altered.

Once the planet has had her say – the process of rebuilding has solid ground on which to do so. The new has a place to flourish. The beginning of the new world becomes the focus, rather than the holding together of a damaged one.

For the abuse, horror, torture and manipulation of Gaia and her people has taken vast quantities of energy from the planet. This is an unseen effect, perhaps, until now. This has taken its toll.

The shift now, the potential energy release now, once it is complete, will astound you.

Words of One

All that has been draining and damaging becomes life supporting and productive. Life is to be encouraged and supported, rather than used as an opportunity for manipulation.

This massive change in focus propels new action and things change rapidly for you with its beginning.

Hold always that the beginning is upon you as well as the ending. This is change and nothing is futile or pointless. All of it is necessary. There will be closure, and this will be helped by a remembering of truth.

It is love and light that moves through Gaia now, healing her, preparing her and fortifying her for the next stage.

Your new world is upon you. Remember this always. This next moment is now called forth in order to begin in fullness and as One.

It will be like nothing you've ever heard. There are notes and instruments unknown that will be freed with this cleansing. They add to the symphony and enrich the song.

The beauty of what awaits you will astound all of your senses, dear human. It is new. It is you. Remember.

That is all.

Thank you.
I have been asked about the vaccines. Would you speak on them?

We have spoken before.

The light quotient matters. Intention matters. Fear has no place in Ascension. Your physical process will not be affected.

All of the actions and reactions by every player, contribute to the whole. Contribute to the Awakening. Contribute to the shift in consciousness.

Fear has no hold here any longer.

Each will choose according to the best outcome at the moment for their own journey.

Your body is a part of this, and contributes to the whole.

There are meant to be many flavors – all contributing now to the whole. Do not buy into the fear. Most of what is heard and seen is propaganda.

Advice on what to do can be summed up in these words – **Do not buy into the fear.**

Fortify yourself with love and light and allow your inner intelligence to dictate your movements. All ways are appropriate, for all are choosing always.

Be pro-active rather than reactive.

Come from love. Trust.

Words of One

Light cures. Light is what you bring to the table. Trust.

That is all.

Thank you.

Goodbye Sophia, my chosen one.

May 6, 2021
6:22 AM

It is the One.

You are now to witness the closing of a chapter of life on Earth. Once it is over, you begin not a new chapter, but a new book. This book will be written by mankind. It will be filled with many wonders and possibilities; things you have labeled as miracles and impossible prior to this moment.

This is the book of the Hue-man.

The abilities you hold are unlocked with this Ascension. This is you, but at a new frequency. The faster vibratory rate into which you are moving allows for more to be done, seen, heard and felt than you've experienced personally.

With the freeing of the race comes complete transformation of the race.

Complete.

The Draco operate most successfully on denser, slower moving planets. Their methods and controls are unsustainable at 5D.

5D is where you are headed.

You are One. The atmosphere into which you move cooperates and supports you, both as you move, and once the move is complete.

Words of One

All of creation conspires with you now, dear human. The difference from that fact alone will astound you. [4]

Allow.
Allow.
Allow.
Allow.

Magic awaits.

Your new world is every dream you've imagined and every wish you've desired.

Trust.
Love.
Hold the light.
It is almost here.

That is all.

Thank you.

Goodbye Sophia, my scribe, my chosen one.

---

[4] *Visual here shows that it is not just "5D" that brings the change. It is* **us**, *in "5D". Combined, it is a powerhouse of a team and the effect expands every part of our lives. Every part.*

Words of One

The End

Made in the USA
Las Vegas, NV
13 October 2021